**Books are to be returned on or before
the last date below.**

12 OCT 2004

28 SEP 2004

**7 – DAY
LOAN**

1 1 OCT 2004

25 OCT 2004

28 SEP 2005

27 OCT 2005

WITHDRAWN

LIBREX

john pawson

john pawson
works

deyan sudjic

I met John Pawson for the first time in 1984 when I was editing a new magazine called *Blueprint*. He had recently abandoned a belated attempt at a formal architectural education at the Architectural Association, and had sent me an envelope full of photographs of a project he had just finished; an art gallery in Cork Street for Leslie Waddington. I had already seen a remarkable apartment of his, published in *World of Interiors*, which caused something of a sensation at the time – especially within the context of the cholesterol-rich, rag roll and dried flowers diet of the pages of that magazine. The photographs showed a home that apparently had nothing in it. Not just no furniture or pictures, but no shelves, no books, no doorknobs, no washing machine, no sofa and no bed – just nothing. The only embellishment had been provided by the photographer, who had positioned, in what was allegedly the kitchen, a thick red slab of beef dripping blood across the stainless steel worktop; an image that took up most of a double-page spread.

The word of mouth about Pawson was exotic. Gossip portrayed him as some sort of lapsed Zen Buddhist monk, an old Etonian who had fled to Japan after frittering away the family fortune. Once there, he had fallen under the spell of Shiro Kuramata, designer of the most beautiful sushi restaurant in the world. He had, so it was said, taken his discipleship to such lengths that, after three months paralysed with indecision about what colour to paint the cornice in his flat, he begged his master to reveal to him the precise shade of pink he should use. It was, of course, just gossip.

The gallery pictures were in black and white and demonstrated Pawson's pursuit of the art of almost nothing, which looked entirely unpublishable. A couple of days after I received the photographs, Pawson telephoned and invited me to come and see the gallery for myself. When we met, there was no sign of the shaven-headed fanatic I had been half expecting, just a dapper thirty-something in a raincoat from Piero de Monzi. We then went to the apartment, which had been carved out of a couple of crudely subdivided rooms in a white stucco terraced house. It was every bit as extraordinary as the *World of Interiors* pictures suggested. Its very emptiness made you acutely aware of how many different shades of white there can be, and of all the nuances and implications of the precise positioning of a door in a wall. The place was not actually as empty as it at first seemed. There were, in fact, futons to sleep on and books and records, but these were neatly stowed behind cupboard doors.

The gallery and apartment were the products, at least in part, of the time that Pawson had spent in Japan, and in particular of the time that he had spent with Kuramata. It was also Kuramata who was responsible for Pawson embarking on an architectural education in the first place. Pawson was never an apprentice, but he had spent all the time that he could in Kuramata's Tokyo office, and he kept in touch when he returned to London. After a couple of projects that Pawson tried to put Kuramata's way failed to materialize, Kuramata turned on his would-be disciple and demanded to know why Pawson didn't get an architectural training and do the work himself.

Kuramata had touched a nerve. 'I was in Bedford Square for some reason, just after he said it, and popped into the Architectural Association. It was just before term started in 1979 and, for a joke, I asked the people behind the reception desk, "Do you have any places left?" and they said, "As it happens, yes we do".'

After a great deal of going back and forth over local authority student grants, Pawson went to school

The Neuendorf House in Majorca (1989, in partnership with Claudio Silvestrin, with whom Pawson worked between 1987 and 1989) was conceived as part of the surrounding landscape; a solid cube set within massive walls.

again at the age of thirty. Unsurprisingly, the experience was not an entirely comfortable one. Under the influence of Bernard Tschumi, the AA tended to place little emphasis on technical skills, such as drafting or engineering. On the other hand, Alvin Boyarsky, the chairman, was a charismatic figure for whom Pawson retains a real respect. The experience was, however, by no means a waste of time; John Andrews and Crispin Osborne – the two tutors that he spent most time with – ended up working with him. The school also gave him the salutary experience of learning to stand up in front of a sceptical jury to defend his work, which is something that has stood him in good stead with even the most difficult of his clients ever since. By the time he was in his third year, however, Pawson had been commissioned to design the gallery for Leslie Waddington in Cork Street, and was ready to set up his own office.

Pawson's was an architecture that was difficult to define in terms of any of the prevailing stylistic camps at the time. For a start, Pawson had never worked for any other architect; he could not be pigeonholed with the High Tech camp, the Postmodernists, or anybody else. It was only when I first travelled to Japan that I began to gain more of an insight into the grounding of Pawson's philosophy. But Japan in general, and Kuramata in particular, were only two among many influences on Pawson: there were the Cistercian ruins at Fountains Abbey, near where he grew up in Yorkshire; there was an abiding interest in simplicity; and a regard for Mies van der Rohe. Pawson was also refreshingly open-minded when talking about his work. His approach was deeply felt, but he never presented what he was doing as any kind of universal solution.

We never did get any photographs that adequately captured the essence of the gallery in a way that

The street frontage of Wakaba restaurant in London (1987) is a single wall of translucent, acid-etched glass providing a barrier between the interior and the outside world. It preserves the tranquillity of the interior, and yet offers a glimpse of the subdued animation of the street outside.

worked for a magazine. In all the best pictures, you found yourself looking at the art; focusing on a prancing Flanagan hare rather than on the architecture. But, of course, that was the whole point of the design, and it demonstrated just how well Pawson had succeeded. *Blueprint* duly published a piece that used words like 'minimalism', perhaps too casually, to describe it. And while Pawson was as close to the art camp as anybody involved in architecture in London at the time, his work could not really be equated with the art movement known as Minimalism. In that context, Minimalism meant the move beyond technique to a conceptual art of ideas. Pawson found art of that kind very interesting; to this day, his office has a Dan Flavin fluorescent on the wall, leaking red light wantonly across the white plaster. His architecture, however, has a different sensibility. In his buildings, technique matters a great deal; the sensual properties of materials and the calculations of proportion matter even more. It is, in many ways, a highly traditional view of what architecture is about. Indeed, Pawson has always seen his work as belonging to an aesthetic strand that links the Cistercian monasteries, the Shaker and Japanese ideas of austerity and contemporary simplicity – which is anything but the denial of the importance of the artist's touch implicit in Minimalism as an art movement.

    This book is the product of time spent in Pawson's office, and of talking with him about architecture, clients and history over several years. I have had the chance to listen to him talking to Calvin Klein about designing a store and watched him showing Cathay Pacific's managers around the airline's new Pawson-designed lounge at Hong Kong International Airport at Chek Lap Kok. We have wandered over the site of Martha Stewart's swimming pool in the Hamptons,

The washbasin from Doris Saatchi's house in London (1988) is a half sphere carved from a single block of white Carrara marble. It marked the beginning of Pawson's interest in designing fixtures and furniture for his interiors.

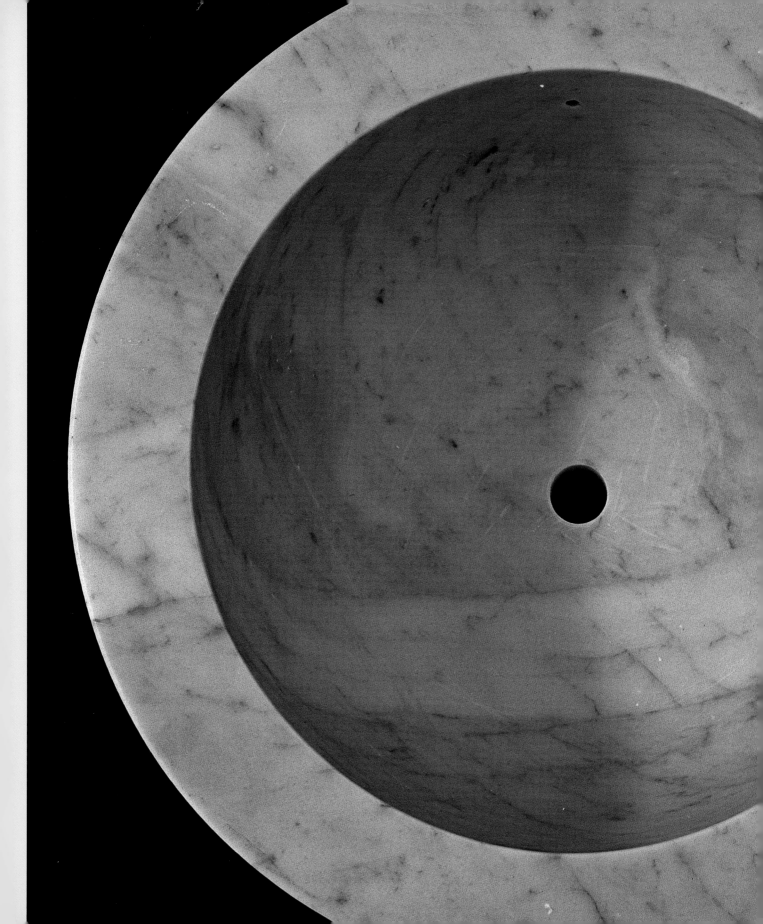

and watched as builders slowly completed the villa that he designed on the island of Majorca. There has been a chance to return, again and again, to the site of his own house in west London – watching the excavation of the basement, the pouring of the concrete frame and the laying of the stone floors – and observe each process gradually coming together to turn the rawness of a building under construction into the carefully crafted finish of architecture.

Over the years, the scale of Pawson's work has increased – a theatre is something very different from a tiny apartment. Similarly, Pawson has begun to attract different kinds of clients. Early on, work came from friends, or friends of friends; a fact which tended to intensify the already charged relationship between architect and client, particularly when the brief was for a home. Even an airline, however, does not approach a commission as an entirely pragmatic process. In fact, from the initial gallery for Leslie Waddington – Pawson's first design for a public space – to work for such determined individuals as Calvin Klein and Martha Stewart, the architect-client relationship has been an important part of every project.

I have talked to Pawson when new commissions have come in, and when they have evaporated – seen success and setbacks. And that long drawn-out process of observation is the basis of this book. The result is, I hope, an exploration of how architecture happens. It is a look at how clients and architects negotiate relationships with each other. It tries to uncover what has gone into the creation of the completed work – the turning points and the motivations – and it examines the meaning of contemporary domesticity.

John Pawson is unusual as an architect in many ways. He came to the subject relatively late, and

The shop front of the Cannelle cake shop in London (1988) was an exercise in display and concealment. The opaque glass facade is punctured in the centre by a clear glass cube, just large enough for the display of a single cake. The indulgence of the pastry is in stark contrast with the simplicity and clarity of the architecture.

he does not have the requisite diploma. But he has managed to create an architecture that presupposes a whole way of life. When his work first started to surface in the 1980s, it was greeted with little less than shock. The restraint, the austerity, and the order and control seemed to run entirely counter to received wisdom about what constitutes domesticity and comfort. And yet, there was something about the beauty of the spaces he made that touched a chord.

His work attracted its partisans and its detractors, but he is without doubt one of the very few architects who have been able to reach a wide popular audience with work that is completely uncompromising. Few of them will ever use a stone bath, own a futon or keep their television set in a cupboard, but they will have been exposed to Pawson's imagery, in magazines, in books, advertising and cinema.

Pawson has managed to transcend the boundaries between art and architecture, between fashion, design and photography. His work is part of a long tradition of simplicity in architecture, and it is longevity which is its strength. It is what gives it a life beyond the fashionable exposure it has enjoyed, and suggests that it will make a lasting impression.

Caught between the smooth plaster walls, the staircase in Pawson's own home provides a seamless upwards movement through the full height of the house.

John Pawson was never meant to be an architect. As far as his father was concerned, his life was to be defined by Eton, Oxford and the family textile business. However, touched by the incendiary spirit of the late 1960s, Pawson left school without completing his final exams, and even though he did his best in the family firm, he was acutely aware that he would never be able to match the business skills of his father.

It was the time spent in Japan that turned him to thinking about architecture; and his connections with the London art world gave him the chance to put those experiences to practical use when he came back from Asia. Pawson had gone to Japan for the first time back in 1973, to escape from the emotional turmoil of an abandoned wedding. In the aftermath, he met someone at a party who offered him a first-class round-the-world ticket for £200, which he accepted without question. Tokyo was his first stop, partly inspired by a fascination with Zen and Japan, and a notion of becoming a Buddhist.

Akira Hayakawa, a karate instructor who had taught Pawson in Chester-le-Street when he was working in the family textile factory nearby, met him at Nagoya airport and introduced him to what was anything but the Japan of the Samurai and tea ceremonies that Pawson had been expecting. Instead, he found himself negotiating a grim landscape of car factories, endless concrete developments with power cables dangling from every available surface, brash neon-lit Pachinko parlours and claustrophobic subways crammed with people.

Pawson, however, was determined to absorb himself in the Japan of his imagination and, upon arrival, insisted on staying at a ryokan. Part of the routine was a diet of fish paste and pickles for breakfast, a damp bed and a nine o' clock curfew. Still, this did not deter Pawson from further exploring his ideas about Buddhism and his genuine attraction to the monastic life. His friend Akira humoured his plans and drove him to one of the most beautiful monasteries in Japan, at Ei-Heiji in the North. While his brief stay at the monastery cured him of his desire to live as a Buddhist monk, Pawson retains a fascination and respect for both the spiritual and aesthetic concepts of Buddhism, which he still draws on for inspiration today.

Having abandoned his plans to become a Buddhist, and without any particular reason to stay, but with no better ideas about what to do, Pawson began teaching at Nagoya University of Commerce, giving English conversation classes to Business Studies students. The money he earned in three years there allowed him to finance a year living in Tokyo. It was here that he picked up a book about Kuramata and realized that it was the same work that had attracted his attention years earlier, when he had seen his designs published in *Domus*. He felt that he had to meet him, and so he simply rang up and introduced himself. 'He was very polite, very generous and very special. He always denigrated his own work; he would take you to the most exceptional and exquisite interior he had done, and all he could say was, "no meaning" or "no sparks".'

Kuramata's modesty extended to his own surroundings; he worked in a crowded studio opening off a simple courtyard in an obscure part of the city. Pawson found himself going back to it as often as he could find an excuse. 'I was a bit too old to become an apprentice, but I did anything I could to be with him … even if it was just to look at the books that he had on his shelves.'

Kuramata was perhaps the first Japanese interior designer to make an international impact, not just with his exquisite interior spaces, but for his furniture as well – no mean achievements given that Japan has yet

MICHAEL YOUNG

to wholly accept the concept of the chair, and didn't even consider using it in the domestic setting until the twentieth century. (His glass chair, for example, with invisible joints, and another piece, made from Perspex into which, by some magical process, he had managed to introduce a scattering of roses.) His interiors, such as his initial store for Issey Miyake in the From First building in Tokyo, and the Esprit store in Hong Kong, were remarkably beautiful, sensuous experiences that had no equal. In their intensity there had been nothing like them since 1907, when Adolf Loos completed the American Bar in Vienna. Pawson was able to see at close quarters Kuramata's brilliant synthesis of the simplicity of traditional Japan with a contemporary aesthetic, and the way in which he was able to abolish the distinction between architecture and design.

When Pawson eventually ran out of money, he went back to Britain and moved to London, where he met Hester van Royen, an art dealer working with Anthony d'Offay. The big step forward for Pawson came when van Royen went to work for Leslie Waddington, London's key gallery owner at the time. By this time, Pawson had spent some time at the Architectural Association and was beginning to find an architectural voice of his own. He designed van Royen's Cork Street office, which Waddington liked, and asked Pawson to design his own. This was followed by another commission for his new gallery a few doors away in Cork Street. It was a project that was vital for Pawson's career. Waddington – an Irish-born dealer, who had operated very successfully from much simpler premises – had come to dominate the twentieth-century London art market. To move into a much bigger space, extending over more than 500m^2 and on two floors, would be making a considerable statement. Pawson believes that his

opposite The Michael Hue-Williams Gallery in Cork Street occupied a shop window at street level to provide a changing showcase for its artworks, while its main space was on an upper floor on the opposite side of the road.

below The short-lived PPOW Gallery, created from a tough industrial interior in New York, had to accommodate exposed heating ducts and a steel structure with maximum economy of means. An upper gallery was accessed through the tall, narrow gap in the wall.

client became increasingly nervous about the whole idea, certainly the relationship became increasingly fraught when Pawson began to work on a design for Waddington's own home. The argument was never about how the gallery looked. Schooled by van Royen's sharply critical eye, Pawson was clear that a quiet, functional space would be appropriate, not an egotistical attempt for the architecture to upstage the art.

Art and architecture are two different things; even if they are producing work that looks, superficially, as if they have more and more in common. Art never has to carry the burden, or the alibi, of utility. The relationship between the two is highly charged and complex; sometimes it can be reduced to nothing more elevated than a turf war. In a gallery, it ought to be clear that it is art that gets pride of place, but this does not always happen. Sometimes, as in the case of the Bilbao Guggenheim, the director pushes the architect, who in any case seldom needs urging, to create a landmark, even though such galleries are often not the most comfortable of spaces in which to show art. It is not surprising, then, that artists should have developed their own views of what constitutes an appropriate setting for art, and it is very rarely a new building. Yet, for an architect, it is not always safe to listen too literally to an artist's wishes. 'When I was doing the Waddington Galleries, Howard Hodgkin genuinely wanted me to paint the walls burgundy, and maybe even burgundy flock, like Dulwich', says Pawson. 'And he wanted me to create a set of arches. What he really meant was that it would be best for his pictures if I did that.'

This was an argument of the kind that Pawson would encounter again when he started designing retail spaces. 'Hodgkin's pictures need small-scale walls to hang on if they are going to look their best. It is just like

opposite and below In the Runkel Hue-Williams Gallery, light, space and the rich, tactile quality of the timber floor provide an environment that subdues the level of background visual noise and compliments the artworks, rather than competing with them. The notched opening allows the receptionist, seated at a desk behind the wall, to have a view into the gallery without intruding into the main gallery space.

merchandising a shop; long interrupted walls make it very difficult to hang a show.'

The Waddington commission, as Pawson perceived it, was not a licence to create art, but a pragmatic issue of getting things right. An art dealer is selling a commodity that is much more cerebral than a piece of clothing, no matter how beautiful, but the detailed functional issues of a commercial art gallery are not so different from the requirements of any retailer. Ultimately, a gallery is a shop, even if most of the actual selling doesn't take place in the gallery's public space. The first stage of the transaction is to view the art, to decide whether to buy or not, and for this reason the gallery needs to make the art look as good, and as potent, as possible. There has to be enough space to stage a changing exhibition, which is what gets a gallery talked about, and room for some stock, in order to actually do business. Much of the business, however, requires private viewing or dealing rooms, as clients don't always choose what they see on the gallery walls, but prefer to select from artworks that the dealer brings into a private room or else from transparencies viewed on a light box.

As Pawson sees it, the fundamental things for the architect to master in a gallery are the floor, the walls and the lighting. And indeed, he has always tried to design the floor so that it is suitable for sculpture; a floor which is fairly neutral, inasmuch as there is no strong and insistent pattern or directional linear arrangement – such as a grid of stone flags, parquet herringbone, or distracting colour or finish. Instead, Pawson's gallery spaces attempt to subdue the level of background visual noise. Sometimes this is achieved with poured concrete, which does away with surface pattern altogether. However, when budgets allow, the floor is often given a richer tactile quality through the use of a softer material, such as

opposite Commercial galleries need exhibition space, storage room for works that are on sale and also areas to negotiate with clients behind the scenes. In the Michael Hue-Williams Gallery, this need for privacy is satisfied with a series of three parallel walls at right angles to the window wall.

below Pawson's remodelling of the interior of the Kerlin Gallery in Dublin makes the most of top lighting to filter daylight directly into the space, while balancing it with a ceiling that appears to float but which can be used to control artificial light.

timber. But here, too, the pattern made by the planks needs careful consideration if it is not to overwhelm the art that stands on it. Another consideration is the way in which the floor meets the wall – an overly elaborate junction, such as a moulded skirting, can compromise the spatial qualities of a gallery that tend to make it sympathetic to works of art. White walls and white ceilings do not compete with artworks. Flexible lighting is imperative if a gallery space is to accommodate multi-media pieces and flatter works on paper, as well as photographs or three-dimensional pieces.

　　　A ground-floor gallery, such as the Waddington Gallery, inevitably has a 'shop window' of some kind, but a large shop window can be distracting from the inside, especially when the entire wall can be seen as part of the outside street scene. Pawson's own instinctive response would have been to minimize the impact of the window, perhaps to make it only semi-transparent. But with the Waddington Gallery, he had also to reckon with his client's commercial instincts. 'Leslie wanted to make sure that people driving past couldn't miss it.' In 1984, when Pawson first took me around the newly completed Waddington Gallery, the large glass window was the dominant architectural experience. It occupied most of the ground-floor facade of the anonymous building in which it was situated. The glass was framed with a minimum of fuss, and pierced by an all but invisible frameless glass door. There was a wooden floor that brought a certain warmth, but had no inherent pattern, and a series of white walls that somehow seemed to float free of the floor. There were also no visible spatial distractions; the stairs, for example, could not be seen from the main space. Here at the Waddington, Pawson had, essentially, made the architecture invisible. There were none of the spatially intense

The Waddington Gallery in Cork Street, Pawson's first major public commission, was designed to be flexible and visually restrained enough to show art of all kinds, from Calder mobiles to figurative work by Flanagan.

experiences that were to characterize some of his later projects, nor could there have been, given the nature of the art gallery brief. In this, and his later gallery projects, Pawson was building up a body of expertise and experience that would be put to use in his later work.

After the Waddington projects, one gallery commission led to another. There was a space in a short-lived storefront gallery for Penny Pilkington and Wendy Olsdorf in Manhattan, known as PPOW in the Lower East Side's Alphabet City area. There was also a gallery for Claus Runkel and Michael Hue-Williams in London which, like Waddington's gallery, was in the West End, but it was off the main street, up several flights of stairs, and therefore a much more introspective and restrained interior. For Hue-Williams he later designed two different spaces, ending up with a gallery that had the advantage of a 5-metre high ceiling, in which he installed a pleasingly worn Japanese oak floor and a bench – an element that he had not previously used in a gallery. There were other projects in Dublin, Frankfurt and for the Henry Moore Foundation at Dean Clough Mills in Halifax. The latter was not a selling space for a commercial dealer, but an exhibition gallery for work produced by the Foundation's residencies programme, and involved working within the fabric of an old carpet mill. Each of them were different projects with different solutions, but over time they allowed Pawson to refine the basic elements of his approach to the gallery, and the relationship of art to architecture.

Alongside the galleries came a succession of art-related projects: a house for the collector Doris Saatchi; a holiday house on Majorca for the German art dealer Hans Neuendorf; a studio for the artist Michael Craig-Martin. Pawson's relationship with van Royen brought with it an instant introduction into the art world.

She introduced him to Donald Judd, an artist who was to become almost as much of an influence as Kuramata. Pawson had met the critic-turned-artist several times, but he regrets that their encounters were not as fruitful as he had hoped they might be. He went out to Marfa, the old army base in a remote corner of south west Texas that Judd had taken over and was gradually transforming into a series of spaces; some explicitly architectural, some installations in which the boundary between art and architecture is not made clear. He learned a lot from Judd's approach, and his way of thinking – his concept of proportion representing 'reason made visible' made a lasting impression. So did the way in which Judd dealt with physical details in his own work. The shadow gap used by Kuramata, that avoids the need for a skirting board, made by leaving a little notch between the bottom of the wall plasterwork and the floor surface, is a solution that appears simple, but actually depends on the skill of the craftsmen involved. Pawson often uses the idea in his own work. But Judd occasionally reversed it, so that the floor is notched a little, to allow a gap around the plaster wall. It is a detail that is all but invisible, yet one which introduces an entirely different spatial dynamic; the emphasis is suddenly on the vertical – rather than the horizontal – and the wall appears to slice through the floor toward infinity. 'Judd made changes to existing buildings which were incredibly subtle, and he was constantly refining. In photographs, you don't always realize how much he has done, but in fact he usually did a lot. He might leave skirtings and floors, but change the ceiling or a junction, or the windows. I have always had this thought of Judd in my mind, and whether he would have wanted to show his work in one of my spaces.'

Judd produced steel and wood artworks that look like furniture, and furniture that looks like art. Both were industrially manufactured, and their quality depended on the skill of the assistants or contractors. Similarly his art is of a scale that can be understood as architecture, and the reverse is also true. To Judd, however, there was never a confusion between them.

Art has changed so much in the past two decades that, according to Pawson, it is now debatable as to whether art should be collectable at all, or if it is, whether it should belong in the home of the individual. Even more fundamentally, the very nature of art itself is under question. Should art be something that endures? Should it even be recognizable as part of an interior space, in the way that paintings or sculpture in the traditional sense once were? Even an attribute as basic as size is now so variable. Much of the current most highly acclaimed work is installational, or site specific; it involves film, video or performance. Such diversity and uncertainty make the task of the architect attempting to design a gallery space, sensitive to the various permutations and intentions of art, increasingly difficult.

'If you give a gallery pristine walls, pristine floors and beautiful details, so that it feels just right, it's an ideal solution from an architectural point of view. But you know that a lot of artists could take exception to that kind of approach. It would make them feel constrained, and they would want to disrupt it. They don't want to show their work in circumstances that feel too comfortable, too pretty or too elegant. You can make simpler spaces, where you take a Georgian interior, say, and just paint it white, leave the existing floorboards, cornice and skirting, and it's not distracting or competitive with the art. I have to work much harder to achieve a sense of visual comfort, without it looking like an installation.'

faggionato apartment

The Piper Building began life as a complex of research laboratories and offices built by the Gas Board, in the days when London still depended for its fuel supplies on publicly owned utility companies. Architecturally, it still betrays those origins, even in its new incarnation as a development of loft apartments. It was a utilitarian structure, but one that acknowledged a certain obligation to the community in its design standards. Now it has closed circuit television cameras constantly sweeping its approaches and a resident concierge. Its wide open interiors have been transformed as more and more newcomers move in; instead of laminates and cheap excuses, it is being fitted out, metre by metre, with travertine and maple, stainless steel and etched glass. In the car park there are BMWs, rather than maintenance vans.

The original steel-frame building was a typical product of the 1960s; a pinwheel complex of high-rise laboratories connected by lower link blocks, and faced in glass curtain walling. As a piece of architecture, it is a conventional functionalist essay of its period, with a lightweight structure clearly expressed on all of its facades. It is competent enough, and not without a certain delicacy for the time, but its most ambitious aesthetic gesture is the giant mural created by the artist John Piper, after whom the building is now named. It is a colourful and decorative work in vitreous panels attached to the exterior of the building; this was municipal modernism at its most high-minded.

What makes the building exceptional is its context. It overlooks a tight bend of the Thames, in the heart of the suburb of Fulham, as it meanders on its increasingly erratic course through London. It stands in an area that has been transformed from working-class inner suburb to rapidly gentrifying enclave. This is

opposite Originally built as a laboratory complex for the Gas Board, the Piper Building's new residential use is signalled by the balconies added to its exterior. The mural, by John Piper, gave the development its new name.

below Interiors that had previously been utilitarian laboratories were subdivided by the developer of the Piper Building to provide shells for individual apartments. Two units were combined to form the Faggionato apartment. It is L-shaped, and contained within the end of the projecting wing of the building.

36

essentially a residential area, but along the river there is a history of industrial sites, wharves, yards and factory sheds; its new function therefore represents an important point of departure.

The nineteenth-century terraced houses that characterize the fine grain of this part of London lap closely around the boundaries of the site, and are dwarfed by the form and size of the Piper complex which looms over them. It is this mismatch of scale that is, in fact, largely responsible for the building's new incarnation as apartments; otherwise, it would, no doubt, have been torn down, or still be standing as a derelict ruin. The Piper is positioned in such a way, and has sufficient bulk, to give it a commanding presence on the west London skyline, visible from long distances in most directions. It affords sweeping open views of the sky, the river and towards central London that would be inconceivable from the windows of any of its diminutive neighbours.

The two-storey terraced houses of this part of Fulham are almost entirely introverted with an outlook that goes no further than the opposite side of the street. They provide a framework for everyday life that is bounded by party walls just 5 metres apart and homes that are the product of tiny cellular layouts. The Piper, on the other hand, with its wide open interior spaces – the result of a structural grid, designed for industrial, rather than domestic uses – allows an entirely different view of space. It is a building that, in any other context, would be entirely ordinary, but it is made into something extraordinary by its position. When the Gas Board moved out, it was acquired by an astute developer who saw the potential of offering large shell apartments, with spectacular views, in a London suburb.

The Piper Building represents, in perhaps the most extreme form, London's increasingly enthusiastic

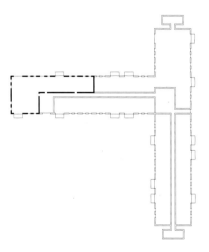

A deep, open-web steel beam was inserted into the existing structure to carry the new mezzanine. It steps back to leave the full-height windows intact. Before the oak floor was laid, the structural concrete floor slab was clearly visible, as were the service pipes and tangled electrical cables.

embrace of the conversion of redundant industrial buildings into residential space. It is a phenomenon that is happening partly because of the inherent spatial qualities of such buildings, but also because of where they are. More and more people are looking to move back into the centre of the city as the new suburbs no longer offer the qualities of urban life that many people identify with. The warehouses of the nineteenth century accommodated the first wave of loft development, partly because they were inexpensive and partly because they were situated in interesting places to live. They were buildings that had their own material qualities: old brick could be sandblasted, inside and out, to give it the texture of corduroy; cast iron structural columns, stripped of generations of paint, look like pieces of sculpture; old wood floors can be sanded and waxed to give them the quality of ancient amber. Indeed, at the end of the 1980s, Pawson worked on just such a loft for Pierre Audi in Oliver's Wharf at Wapping.

The Piper Building was a different proposition. There was no romantic Victorian engineering to work with, just an open, column-free and somewhat clinical, antiseptic structure. Its palette of materials was comparatively insipid and flimsy to the point of banality. What the Piper undoubtedly did have in its favour, however, was a series of remarkable views and some enormous spaces; a combination which makes this a rather different kind of loft development. Security is certainly an issue; the Piper building is surrounded by high fences, defending its car park from theft, and protecting the endless corridors that serve the apartments from unwelcome intruders. Its residents tend to be more affluent and older than their Clerkenwell counterparts, and they are more likely to have children and to need large spaces.

The Piper has already seen commissions for its interiors go to a number of leading designers including Ron Arad. Pawson was asked to design a home for an art dealer, Anne Faggionato, and her financier husband Mungo Park. They had known Pawson for some time, and knew that this new home would mean an entirely new way of life. Faggionato's previous home had been a very traditional flat near Kensington Square. The move required a new approach to domestic habits, new ways of dealing with possessions, new ways for the couple to relate to each other and to their children. It also involved acquiring a alternative selection of furniture; their old furniture would look very different in such a carefully considered interior.

The architect was aware of a certain initial reserve from his clients. Faggionato later told Pawson that when she had shown her mother a book about his work, her response had been sceptical, 'You spend all that money to look poor?' In fact, the relationship between Pawson and his clients developed very smoothly. And, after seeing a model of the apartment, Faggionato declared it to be just what she wanted, with only the minimum of modifications.

The apartment is enormous. Faggionato bought two units and combined them to form an L-shaped interior; at 600m², it is the size of three or four conventional terraced houses. The entrance hall has enough room to accommodate the entire floor plan of Pawson's own house. In the short arm of the 'L', the unit runs the whole thickness of the slab block with triple aspect windows, offering a long view westward up river, south across the river and north over Fulham. The long arm of the 'L' is single aspect, looking out over the north side of the slab. There are few historical precedents for living in this way. Purpose-built housing very rarely has

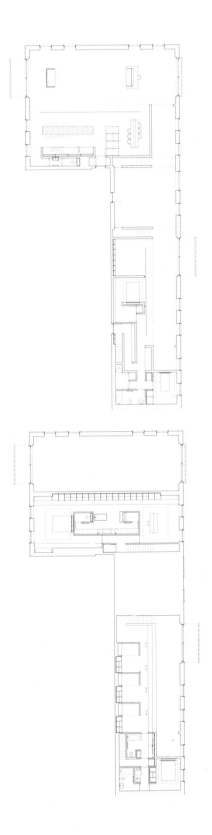

opposite The new materials, in particular the oak floors, offer a warmth that was previously absent. From the main level, the children's bedrooms are invisible. The sheer length of the uninterrupted space along the window wall provides a counterpoint to the living room, which turns the corner at the far end.

left The apartment was created by combining a pair of shell units, an arrangement which provides two entrances. The front door opens into an entrance hall; the back door allows for a secondary staircase that leads directly to the children's bedrooms. The upper, mezzanine, level is punctured with voids to allow for double-height spaces; one over the living area, another over the entrance hall and the whole length of the window wall.

The three children's bed-
rooms share a mezzanine
deck overlooking the dou-
ble-height slice of space in
front of the windows. Two
deep shelves, stepped one
above the other, form a
work bench which they can
all share.

previous page   The living
room, with its oak floor
laid in random lengths, is
related to, but not a part
of the dining room and
kitchen, which are both
obscured behind a glass
screen. The simplicity and
tactile quality of the completed apartment is the
product of the skill with
which the messy banality
of the underlying structure
can be tamed and enriched
by new surfaces.

floor plans of this kind; nor does it, generally speaking, have ceiling heights just tall enough to accommodate a mezzanine level. Pawson has deliberately not interfered with the sense of endless space. You walk into the main entrance hall, which comes as a powerful sense of relief after the endless corridors snaking through the building from the main entrance, and find yourself in a space which is simply breathtaking. The north wall is also full height, its windows marching for more than 35 metres across the facade, as if it were the Versailles of lofts.

The oak floor is laid in random widths to give it a rhythm and to give the interior the tactile material quality it previously lacked. The subdivision was relatively easily mapped out. The living room occupies the full-height section of the short arm of the 'L' with the west-ward view. Its kitchen, measuring 15 metres by 6 metres, and dining room are accommodated under the mezzanine, which is itself screened from the main living area by a smoked glass wall. The kitchen, with its Pawson-designed Obumex fittings, occupies the majority of this compartment, stopping short of the perimeter wall.

Upstairs, on the mezzanine, the ceiling height of the main bedroom is just enough to accommodate its new use. A six-footer will clear the ceiling, but lie on the bed and you have a grandstand view south to overlook the river. The bathroom is a free-standing island in the middle of this space, which defines the extent of the study at the rear and insulates it from the sleeping area. Floors are oak throughout, and the tub is an oak-faced box, lined with cedar, which can better withstand prolonged contact with water.

The plan maintains and exploits the full height of the structure for almost the full length of the apartment, and fits in the mezzanine level at the rear of the long arm of the 'L'. It is an arrangement which allows

The dining room and kitchen are accommodated under the mezzanine in the short arm of the 'L', and screened from the main living area by a smoked glass wall.

for the privacy of the parents, who have a self-contained bedroom, bathroom and study accessed by their own staircase. A second mezzanine provides three bedrooms, opening off an open gallery, with another self-contained bedroom and bathroom on this level for the live-in housekeeper. Underneath this gallery is a TV room, a guest bedroom, and a further self-contained bedroom and bathroom.

The mezzanine was an essential element to make the plan work, both for an appropriate level of privacy and subdivision. It allows for conventional self-contained bedrooms, as well as more open arrangements. The result is a sequence of spaces unusual in a loft: a proper entrance hall, with all the necessary characteristics for showing artworks; the long gallery running the length of the north wall, which is ideal for entertaining; and a further living room and dining room – spaces that are not immediately apparent to the visitor.

Pawson's design solution manages to be practical, but also visually compelling. With the carefully designed skirting detail – a notch in the oak floor, to allow white walls to slice unfettered through the space – there is a sense of finely-tuned, tautly controlled space throughout the apartment.

calvin klein

Architecture is a concept that slips into conversations about fashion surprisingly often. It crops up when people try to talk about cut and cloth and find themselves rapidly running out of vocabulary. A few particularly celebrated fashion designers are even spoken of respectfully as being 'architectural' in their approach. But fashion is not, or at least was not until very recently, a word that architects could feel comfortable with. They tend to regard fashion as an essentially ephemeral phenomenon, and they consider themselves to be engaged in a more fundamental, if not a more serious endeavour, one whose outcome is meant to last. Inasmuch as it impinges on the consciousness of the fashion world at all, architecture as it really is – rather than 'architecture' as a conveniently portentous adjective – is seen as slow and ponderous, a response tinged by a certain sneaking envy. Neither field have so far ranked high on a cultural pecking order that has traditionally been dominated by literature, music, drama and art. Of the two, architecture has enjoyed a more elevated status; certainly it has achieved a critical literature, which is more than can be said of fashion.

There is a misunderstanding between the two camps, a mismatch in perceptions that has verged on institutionalized hostility. Architects enjoy the kind of self-regard that comes from seeing themselves as being involved with cultural issues wider than simple commerce. And yet, at the same time, they have looked on jealously as fashion's strengthening grip on the popular imagination has eclipsed them as taste makers. Fashion, on the other hand, has secretly craved some of the cultural credibility that comes from the heavyweight baggage that architecture brings with it. The typical fashion designer may not know exactly what the Bauhaus was, but he or she has at least heard of it.

Partly, this mismatch is to do with different timescales. Three months is an eternity in the frenetic fashion year, with its constant demands for fresh material to fill the aching void that two annual collections represent for any designer. Architecture is lucky not to look hopelessly out of date by the time it has negotiated the treacle-like speed of the construction process, counted in years rather than weeks. After a brief interlude of a decade or so when they may, or may not, look contemporary, most buildings must endure another quarter of a century in which they are regarded as hopelessly outmoded. Then, if they are lucky, the best of them may eventually be understood for their intrinsic qualities, rather than through the filter of any particular stylistic language. Architecture, despite all sorts of attempts to prove otherwise, from high-tech notions of built-in obsolescence to postmodernism, is meant to last, to be about the big things. Fashion, on the other hand, is presented as being about the allegedly trivial and frivolous, concerned with nothing more than seasonal fads. Certainly it does not age well; haute couture turns into stained and faded old clothes with brutal rapidity.

When fashion has picked up clues from architecture, the reaction from the architectural camp has typically moved from the initial sense of charmed surprise to unease that comes from the dismaying realization that what fashion takes up, it can discard again, leaving it worn out and stripped of meaning. Le Corbusier put the sense of barely concealed mutual antagonism into words when he suggested that style in architecture was of no more significance than the feathers on a woman's hat, pretty enough but of no real importance. The truth is that fashion is anything but trivial; it is about such undeniably fundamental aspects of life as sex, status and identity. It even tracks the passing

of the seasons, reinforcing the belief that we need different outfits to deal with summer and winter. It has become a vast international industry that keeps entire economies buoyant, as textile mills spill out miles of cloth, and garment factories churn out running shoes, shirts and jeans by the million. What is more, fashion has taken on the fabrication of imagery with the deadly seriousness of a science. In the end, fashion is about emotional resonances even more than it is about the physical issues of cloth, cut, silhouette and texture. Because of this preoccupation with imagery, fashion has fuelled media in every form; cinema, print, video, as well as music. Fashion designers have shaped the way that each succeeding decade has defined itself. Through the catwalk and the collections, with their carefully choreographed hierarchy of the seating plan and the endless photo opportunities, it has provided an arena in which ideas of glamour and celebrity have been communicated internationally and instantly, as powerfully as Hollywood or the music business.

The real difference between fashion's role in the contemporary world, in comparison with any previous period, is the way in which a handful of stars have managed to put the focus on their own names, rather than on any specific garment. Through the skilful manipulation of graphic design, packaging, photography and publicity, a fashion signature becomes a brand capable of the alchemical transformation of virtually anything it touches, from the humblest pair of socks to an entire outfit.

When we buy fashion, practical considerations do not figure high on the agenda. People who shop in Bond Street, the via della Spiga or Rodeo Drive are not primarily in search of a means of keeping dry or warm. If we wear garments that come from these places, it is

previous page The Madison Avenue Calvin Klein store was formerly an austere, neoclassical bank. The pilasters that once defined the bank are still intact, their impact subtly reinforced by the new glazing pattern. The Klein name is discreet, but the store still has a commanding presence on its corner site. It offers a calm retreat from the busy street.

because of the dreams that come with them. For a moment, they give us the sensation that we are part of the surprisingly complete world that the designer has conjured up. The essence of fashion is in the way that it can trigger emotional responses; anything from nostalgia and glamour, to exoticism and toughness. Where architecture does have an important part to play in this process is to create a setting that brings to life the dreams associated with the character of a fashion brand.

Calvin Klein is certainly among the most respected of the current crop of America's fashion designers. If Ralph Lauren has carved out for himself a nostalgic territory that is based on wistful memories of old moneyed WASP style, Klein has made the idea of modernity all his own. His body-conscious clothes – austere, simple and yet sensual and assured – have helped to define a way of life. While he has always had a masterful command of the detail of clothing, as well as a brilliant way with the of-the-moment advertising that supports his products, he was relatively late in establishing a retail flagship. Until the early 1990s, Klein sold his various ranges and licensed accessories through independent retailers, rather than set up his own network of stores. As such, it was the department stores that determined how Klein looked to his customers. His peers, designers such as Issey Miyake, Rei Kawakubo, Giorgio Armani and Ralph Lauren, had already invested in the creation of flagship stores in which, with the artifice of a theatre production, they were able to deploy every element of their work in one place, in command of the whole look. The clothes, the packaging, the display techniques, the rituals of salesmanship, the advertising, all came together, with the architecture, to create a synthesis of what the brand is about.

It was the creation of such a place that Klein had in mind when he started to negotiate for, what was still, a bank building on a prominent corner of Madison Avenue at East 60th Street. It was a move that was to transform the nature of Klein's business, to say nothing of Manhattan's social geography. This part of Madison Avenue had previously been largely untouched by fashion; it was an enclave of corporate offices and hotels. Since his arrival, a host of other retailers have followed him into the area with high profile outlets of their own.

Klein was looking for an architect whose approach would reflect his own preoccupations, somebody who could help him create the architectural equivalent of his collections. This was going to be more than a simple shop, it was going to say something about Calvin Klein's values, and to provide a point of reference for other Klein stores to come around the world. So it was that, after having seen a copy of a book about Pawson given to him by Ian Schrager, he found himself outside his basement office close to London's Tottenham Court Road in autumn, 1993. Pawson remembers the day well. 'Klein arrived with Rick Rector, the company's vice president. "I saw your book, I loved the work", was all Klein said as he shook hands. Rector was a little more explicit, "We are thinking of doing a store in New York" he offered by way of explanation for their sudden appearance.' At the time, most of Pawson's architectural work was centred on galleries and domestic projects, but that was not necessarily a handicap in Klein's eyes. There is a lot of common ground between a gallery – a quiet, unobtrusive background to art – and a setting for the kind of clothes that aspire to something close to the status of art. The fact that Pawson was not associated with other high-profile fashion retailers was, in some ways, also a plus. It meant that his work would be specifically identified with Klein.

Fitting the full-height glass panels, that distinguish the Calvin Klein store in New York, required heavy lifting gear, and the closure of the road outside over a weekend. Despite the muscular equipment, the result is a subtle transformation of the exterior of the building.

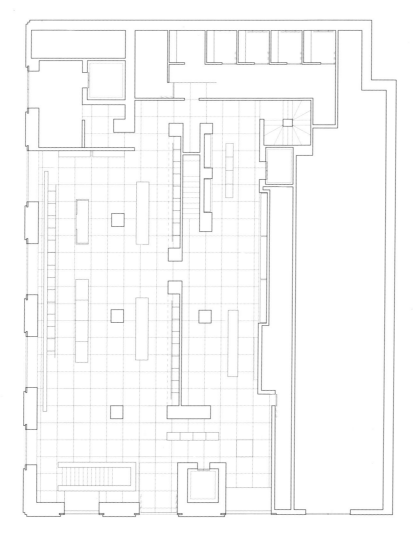

opposite and left When Klein first brought Pawson to the Madison Avenue store, it was still a bank with a lofty banking hall compromised by mundane later additions. The upper level, inserted by Pawson, steps away from the windows to allow for a spectacular sense of space. This level is devoted to women's wear displayed on mannequins, or hung on carefully fabricated rails.

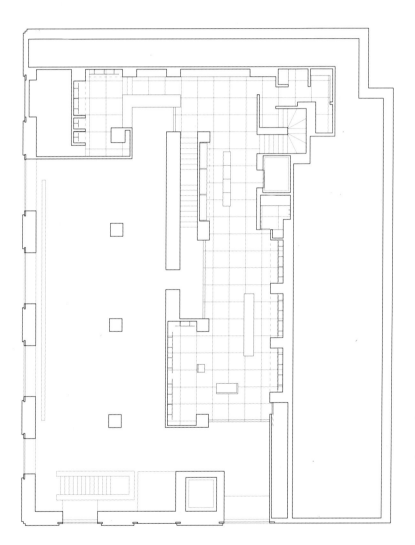

opposite and left Klein
was initially concerned
about the visual impact of
the original internal
columns, but with the load
of 20 floors above them,
they had to stay. The store
layout is designed to minimize their impact. The new
insertions retain the lofty
proportions of the interior
at the window walls.
Madison Avenue needed to
accommodate the full
upper end of the Klein
range – men and women's
clothes, as well as home-
ware, shoes and underwear
– and each collection needed its own distinct area.
Pawson's plan ensured
that each related clearly to
the rest, rather than making them self-contained
incidents.

Pawson had already designed one fashion shop, RK RK on the Brompton Road. It had not lasted for long, and all traces of it had been gutted by the time Klein met Pawson, but it had been published and had attracted Klein's attention. It had been built to a restricted budget, but Pawson had created an interior that looked fresh and out of the ordinary in the overheated context of retail design of the late 1980s. The street front was a frameless sheet of glass, set directly into the floor and walls. There was no window display, and the basement level had the quality of an archaeological find, with its austere monumental vaults. The clothes were ordered into displays that concentrated on individual garments, rather than on showing them in bulk. There was nothing left to see at the site of RK RK, but there was a new apartment that Pawson had just finished for the art dealer, Hester van Royen, on the Chelsea embankment. Sitting at her kitchen table, Klein began to talk about the neo-classical bank in New York that he was interested in, and about his own approach to design. He repeated the words 'modern' and 'simple'.

This was not the first time that Pawson had considered the detailed issues of fashion. In the 1960s, he had worked in one of his father's Tyneside textile factories, making clothes that appealed to the buyers of a string of provincial stores – a world away from the direction that fashion has taken since then. Pawson attempted to modernize the company with a new collection, and he even designed a short-lived London showroom himself. His background gave him a certain insight into Klein's approach. 'Working with Calvin, I began to understand that he saw architecture very much in the same way that he saw the process of fashion design. Designing clothes, you work with a room full of pattern cutters who interpret drawings, and if you are Calvin, you can come in

and get them to cut bits of the toile until they have got it
right. There were times when it was like that with the
Madison Avenue store. He wanted to get involved with
the design in the same way, but of course carving marble
is not like pattern making, you just can't put the bits back
when they have come off – I wish you could.'

Calvin Klein's business has a turnover
measured in hundreds of millions of dollars. His head-
quarters occupy seventeen large floors of an office
building in Manhattan. There are mock-up display units,
rooms full of publicists and desks at which buying teams
negotiate on price. He has outlets all over Asia, America
and Europe, but the business is run with a distinctly individual touch. It is based on Klein's personality, without
any of the dilution that comes from a corporate management style. 'When you are with Calvin, you quickly for-
get just how powerful he is, the size of his business, the
buying power he has, the fame he has acquired. The
knock-on effect he has on other businesses is huge.
There are so many other people's lives bound up with
what he decides to do', says Pawson.

Pawson's first conversation with Klein was
the start of a continuing relationship that has waxed
and waned in its intensity, but which has changed the
architect's career. Klein has been Pawson's most important client in enabling him to move on from concentrating on the small-scale interior. He has taken Pawson
from Madison Avenue to Seoul, and from Paris to the
Bluewater shopping centre, the last of Britain's mega
malls on the edge of London's orbital M25 motorway.
Klein's retail outlets have expanded across the world, as
he has unveiled a variety of different retailing formats,
from his inexpensive jeans line to his main brands.

The Madison store was to involve a long,
drawn-out design process, partly as a result of Klein's

need to feel convinced that he was on the right course.
While Pawson had a strong stylistic sympathy for Klein's
minimalist ethos, he had as much to learn about the
mechanics of retailing as Klein. Given the cost of each
precious square foot of mid-town Manhattan space, this
could not simply be a piece of retail sculpture, it had to
work in commercial terms. At the same time, Pawson
had his own objectives; the project was an opportunity
for him to move into new territory. The challenge was to
meet the technical demands of a shop, without compro-
mising the aesthetic vision. Could it be done without
diluting the intensity of Pawson's architecture? Pawson
tried to bring the quiet refinement of simple materials, a
restricted palette and the suppression of the visually
superfluous to the project. He went to great lengths to
omit the clutter of the grilles and ducts that are so
ubiquitous to conventional retail interiors that they are
mistakenly considered to be invisible. He wanted to
maintain the dignity of the proportions of the interior
as much as possible.

In the early stages, there were endless conversations between Klein and Pawson. 'When you ask,
"Calvin what is your collection about this time?", he
says "its kind of modern, kind of sexy, it's about a new
idea of luxury".' Actually, what he really does is create
the conditions in which people feel good about spend-
ing money. He wants surroundings that don't seem
ostentatious, or overtly luxurious, so people don't feel
guilty about going in.'He has incredible energy and
drive, and is very focused. He will shut off when the conversation veers away from his direct business interests.
I talked a lot about Donald Judd when we were dis-
cussing the interior, but it took a long time to persuade
him that he should fly out to Marfa in Texas, and see
Judd's work for himself.'

A clothes shop imbued with the status and ambition of Calvin Klein has a certain amount in common with an art gallery. At the Tokyo Calvin Klein outlet, as with all the stores, the aim is to create architecture that makes the most of the content. In the retail world, the eternal problem is to minimize the impact of the air conditioning grilles, emergency lighting and loudspeakers that conventionally turn even the most carefully considered interiors into cluttered and distracting foreground, rather than neutral background.

The store consists of two spaces linked by three broad steps used for display areas.

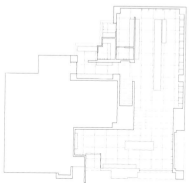

The New York shop was originally planned to open in August 1994, but as things turned out, it took two years from that first meeting in London to the opening party. Along the way, there were endless conversations about how far a shop for Calvin Klein could diverge from the retail norms, and periods of doubt and questioning. Klein had never opened a shop before; it was a move he knew would be minutely scrutinized, not just by the press and his customers, but also by his competitors. Architecture was new territory for him, and he was feeling his way with caution. Model after model was made, carefully photographed and shipped back and forth over the Atlantic.

One year after meeting Pawson, Klein hired Gabriella Forte, once Giorgio Armani's right-hand woman, to help develop the business. Her off-the-cuff response to Pawson's design, by this time ready to go out to tender, was that it was too soon to open a store in Manhattan as the systems to run it simply weren't in place. The process seemed to stall, and the project's site start date was delayed and delayed.

Then came the chance to do a franchise store for Klein's Japanese partners in Tokyo, right across the street from the Commes des Garçons flagship. Madison Avenue was never meant to be a detailed model for every new Klein store. The plan was that each design would be a response to specific circumstances, which was how the Tokyo store was designed. Unfortunately, it was in an unprepossessing red brick building, one of those curious new developments that their builders fondly and mistakenly imagine symbolize sophistication on the basis of a pediment and a classical doorway. Pawson did his best but, without the budget to travel for regular site supervision, the interior didn't turn out to be quite what Klein had been expecting, particularly in terms of lighting.

Fashion is a global phenomenon. The emerging markets of Asia have provided some of the most important customers for western designers. Japan was first in the field, with Hong Kong and Singapore close behind. Now it is countries like Korea that are adopting global fashion. In Seoul, the Calvin Klein store gave Pawson a chance to create not just an interior, but to shape the exterior of the building with a facade that uses the same stone as the floor and the entrance steps.

Work slowly continued on the Madison Avenue project, until the day that Klein came up with the idea of involving interior designer and personal friend Joe D'Urso, who had designed an interior for Esprit in Los Angeles in the 1980s. D'Urso would, said Klein, be just the person to help with the furniture and colour scheme. At first, Pawson thought this was a positive idea. After a series of conversations, D'Urso began unrolling more and more rolls of yellow detail paper and putting forward his own ideas about reorganizing Pawson's plan for the store. 'Joe wanted the shop to consist of lots of little vignettes, he tried to make each corner of the shop into a still life. He created a lot of cul-de-sacs that broke the flow, and made it very un-simple'. The impasse was eventually resolved by Gabriella Forte. 'She said to me, "You have three options; you walk away, you shut up or you fight your corner".' Pawson thought about it and decided to stay with the project, and it was D'Urso who finally left. Despite the second guessing, Klein was committed to working with Pawson, and he had no desire to end up with a reputation for walking off jobs.

The questions that remained to be resolved were about the circulation. 'We were never going to have escalators, but where did the lift go? And where would the stairs, fit?' As the project took detailed shape, Klein began to look at the emerging design and to ask questions about the fundamentals of the structural layout. Once the contractors had started on site, he would go in and start arranging the fittings, wanting to take out rails anchored to the wall, or a glass shelf that had taken two weeks to fit.

The Madison Avenue store has now become one of New York's landmark retailing interiors, and the lasting impression is of space and silence within the busiest of urban contexts. The handsome neoclassical

opposite and below Seoul ground floor plan and interior. At the Seoul outlet Pawson used a grey stone for the floor, a strong visual base for the store, which effectively brings the street indoors – an idea that was first put forward for the Manhattan store.

structure has been subtly transformed by the deft inser-
tion of pavement-to-fourth-floor panels of glass that
have the effect of apparently putting the whole building
into a showcase. Their installation appears as though it
must have been effortless, but it actually involved a
great deal of orchestration; the street intersection was
closed to traffic for one weekend to allow the glass to be
craned into position. Inside, through the 6-metre high
glass vestibule, the immediate impression is of stone
floors – square sand-coloured Yorkstone flags now worn
to the finish of cashmere – and meticulous precision. On
a stifling August day, the noise and dust of the city fades
away as you step into the cool double-height entrance
area. A staircase rising up to the mezzanine defines the
main floor into two distinct areas, above which stone
benches seem to float. It is a plan that allows for a series
of distinct spaces. It does not reveal itself all at once, and
yet you do not feel manipulated or subject to confusing
spatial gimmickry. Here and there are individual Pawson
pieces – a marble basin, a douglas fir bed – used to
establish the home collection. This is an interior that is a
setting for fashion that sets itself apart from the everyday by its discretion and its grace, rather than by ostentation or striving for effect.

After the opening, Klein told Pawson, 'I visit
the shop every day, and it always makes me feel good.'
He returned to Pawson for a job in Seoul in 1996. This
was not just an interior, but a free-standing building
which involved an external architectural treatment. For
the floor he used a grey stone, a strong visual base for
the store, which in effect brings the street indoors, an
idea that Pawson had first put forward for Manhattan.
The same stone was applied to the external elevations.

Pawson then designed the Calvin Klein Jeans
system, used to furnish franchise stores devoted to the

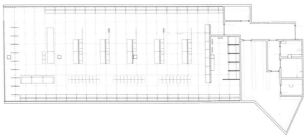

most inexpensive of Klein's ranges. Customers are likely to be younger and have less disposable income than those for other Calvin Klein labels. Space and budgets are more restricted, but the stores do not condescend to them. The design, a kit of parts using metal mesh, etched acrylic and wood furniture inserted within a wood or stone envelope, can work in malls as well as buildings with more individual architectural character, and distils the essence of the CK identity. Jeans are no longer utilitarian workwear; Klein uses denim as a sensuous, highly tactile material, and the stores communicate that. The first opened in 1999 at the Bluewater shopping centre just outside London.

According to both Klein and Pawson, the process of working together over several years has involved a genuine exchange. 'People feel that, with my work, it is not a collaboration, but actually it is', says Pawson. 'Just as a site dictates what is going to come out of the situation, so clients give you ideas. I have come to feel that, taking Calvin on balance, he was mostly right about the things that worried him in the Madison Avenue shop. He likes contrast, he likes dark furniture in a natural white space. He likes stone that has no fossil whorls or taints because, as far as he is concerned, it makes stone as modern as concrete. You have an idea in your mind about what you want to do but decisions aren't made in a cool reflective way in the studio; they get made in a corridor, in a boardroom, and everyone in the organization has an opinion. He is a creative guy, but I try to stick up for myself.'

Floor plan and window display of the CK Jeans outlet at the Bluewater shopping centre just outside London. The CK Jeans range is cheaper, and aimed at a younger audience than Klein's couture range, and they sell in different settings. Pawson was asked to design an approach to the jeans stores that could be applied to a variety of environments, including malls, such as Bluewater. The look is clearly different from the bigger Klein stores, but it still aims for a sense of modernity and glamour.

obumex kitchen

Herman Muthesius, author of the influential book *Das Englische Haus*, and a critic who helped to popularize the simplicity and directness of English domestic Arts and Crafts architecture, once claimed that the English were not interested in 'show or comfort' in the kitchen. His explanation was that in Britain, 'middle-class housewives never cross the threshold of the kitchen', unlike their German counterparts, 'who regarded the kitchen as their concern and arranged it lovingly throughout.' Certainly, in the first half of the century, kitchens and laundries were the preserve of servants, not their masters. Even in the iconic houses that have defined the modern movement, spatial and social innovation mostly stopped at the pantry door. The kitchen was often regarded as if it were the engine room of a ship; another world, populated by crew rather than passengers.

The design of the kitchen was treated very much as the interior of a garage is today, a piece of pragmatic and utilitarian design more than an aesthetic statement. The interior was characterized by raw finishes, exposed service runs and dominated by appliances – just as even the most elaborate contemporary architectural landmarks, such as museums or theatres, quickly run out of architectural ambition beyond their public spaces. Often, the industrial quality of the kitchen was fully justified on functional grounds; it was a place that processed food as well as prepared it for the table.

The culture of the kitchen has now been turned upside down. Food shopping is done once a week in bulk and a large refrigerated storage space is a necessity to accommodate it. Food preparation has become less the central purpose of a kitchen, superseded by its function as, principally, a social space. The formal drawing room, as well as the dining room, have steadily lost ground as elements in the planning of the middle-class home. By the end of the twentieth century, the kitchen has become not just indisputably part of the upstairs world, but symbolically the centre of the home. The kitchen has become the place in which conversation and entertaining tends to take place. It is the preserve not just of the family, but the place in which their friends and visitors are welcomed. The removal of intervening walls has given it the possibility of a greater architectural complexity. Even the very rich now have a kitchen at the centre of their house, although there may be another more utilitarian kitchen in which the staff work.

In today's climate, while food has become a subject of all-pervading interest, the actual preparation of food at home has become less and less common. We watch television chefs on every channel, we devour the columns of restaurant critics in the newspapers; but in the supermarket it is the ready-prepared meals that take up most space. We eat out more often, and not just for special occasions; it is a phenomenon that encompasses the expensive restaurant as well as fast food, and week-day breakfasts as much as Sunday lunches. Yet we remain wedded to the idea of the kitchen, almost as a symbolic commitment or tribute to values that no longer shape our lives. The kitchen has become a commodity. It is manufactured and sold as an entity discrete from the rest of the house. It has been designed stylistically to embody certain values; warmth, domesticity, tradition, on one side, efficiency, or fashion, on the other. Domestic appliances have been turned into consumer products, branded and styled with new models coming out every year, just like motor cars. Refrigerators, and ovens in particular, have grown larger and larger; the simplest refrigerator is now two metres high and contains a deep freeze and an ice maker. We have seen the phenomenon of the so-called 'professional' kitchen.

The domestic kitchen, so we are led to believe, now needs the best possible chef's knife made from hollow ground carbon steel. It needs a kitchen range that could do service in a restaurant kitchen dealing with 200 covers a day. Electric orange squeezers have to be able to produce a gallon of juice at a time; toasters must be capable of despatching half a dozen muffins at once. And to dispose of the by-products of all this conspicuous consumption, we have sinks equipped with electronic waste disposal units and powerful air extractor fans.

All this is a long way from the domestic world envisaged by the first architect of note to have designed a kitchen with a general application. The Viennese-trained architect Margarete Schutte-Lihotsky designed the Frankfurt Kitchen in 1924 for social housing built by the progressive civic authorities in that city. It was designed to make the most out of every inch of space in the very restricted apartment kitchen, in order to make domestic life function more easily; it was characterized by neat rows of bins to store flour, coffee, sugar, spices and racks on which to dry and store dishes, pots and pans. The work surfaces were carefully designed to be easily cleaned, and she even devised a prefabricated concrete sink. The relationship of larder to stove and sink, based on Fordist research to systemize industrial work on production lines, was carefully considered; the kitchen became a functionally organized process rather than a collection of pieces of furniture.

Shutte-Lihotsky was working for people who would now be considered poor, but her innovations have shaped all kitchens ever since, and the Frankfurt model can be regarded as the ancestor of every fitted kitchen that there has ever been. Since the 1920s, the kitchen has gone through an accelerated evolutionary

The curve is an unusual motif in Pawson's aesthetic repertoire. The simple tubular steel spout has been scaled up for functional, as well as stylistic, reasons. It enables a more efficient means of directing water flow between adjacent sinks and it also provides a sculptural signature for the Obumex kitchen.

process. It has veered from loose furniture to built-in installations and back again. The process of functional planning that Shutte-Lihotsky embarked on has turned into a science. Yet, underneath the rational justifications, the kitchen is still an environment governed as much by emotional concerns as functional issues.

The kitchen system that Pawson designed for the Belgian company Obumex is aimed at a very different audience from the one that Shutte-Lihotsky had in mind. It is expensive; a luxury in fact. It is also designed on a scale that reflects how much more important, and how much bigger the kitchen has become as an element in the house. More often than not, the Obumex kitchen is found in houses that have already had a kitchen, rather than in completely new buildings. The process is a reflection of the way that, when we move home, the existing kitchen may be perfectly serviceable, but we like to install our own just the same. It is a phenomenon that suggests that, although kitchens look more as if they are part of the architectural background, they are in fact pieces of furniture. And as such, we like to make our own choices about how they should look.

Pawson first encountered Obumex when he was giving a lecture about his work in Antwerp. Afterwards, a couple of people from the company introduced themselves and said that they would like to discuss the possibility of Pawson designing a showroom for them. A long drawn-out courtship process ensued and it eventually transpired that what the company really wanted was a new kitchen design. It took a couple of years for those conversations to turn into a real commission. Pawson had designed pieces of furniture before, but this was the first chance that he had to create a new product that would be made in quantities. It was a much more complex and elaborate brief than a simple chair. At

The Pawson-designed halogen hobs are set flush into the surface of the work-top and are operated by steel lever controls of the same design as those that are used to control the water flow.

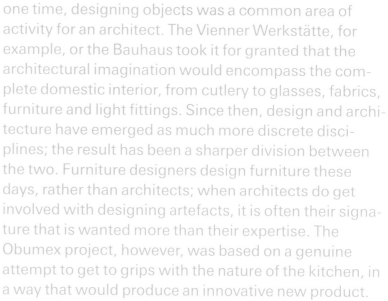

one time, designing objects was a common area of activity for an architect. The Vienner Werkstätte, for example, or the Bauhaus took it for granted that the architectural imagination would encompass the complete domestic interior, from cutlery to glasses, fabrics, furniture and light fittings. Since then, design and architecture have emerged as much more discrete disciplines; the result has been a sharper division between the two. Furniture designers design furniture these days, rather than architects; when architects do get involved with designing artefacts, it is often their signature that is wanted more than their expertise. The Obumex project, however, was based on a genuine attempt to get to grips with the nature of the kitchen, in a way that would produce an innovative new product.

Established in 1960, Obumex began modestly by manufacturing school furniture. It did not take long for the company to branch out into high quality kitchens – its focus was on innovation and tailor-made solutions for individual clients, a bespoke approach that it likens to haute couture. The company's decision to work with Pawson reflects its intention to add, what might be described – using the same fashion analogy – as a diffusion range to its made-to-measure collection, more widely available to clients through suitable distributors, as well as direct from the company. Neither its existing products nor the collaboration with Pawson is about the fleetingly fashionable. However; Obumex has prided itself on making simple, timeless products, built to last. They compare, with justice, their values to those expressed by the products of such companies as Porsche and Chanel. The collaboration with Pawson was to establish a range of kitchen designs that brought together the principles and discipline of his architecture and to apply it to a range of products.

The basic units have a worktop made of either steel, timber, Carrara marble or, as above, lava stone. The system can be set against a wall or, as here, free-standing. Open shelves are used in conjunction with drawers concealed behind the flat plane of the unit front. The unit pulls out to reveal several drawers inside.

opposite Drawers can be customized with timber organizers, in this case walnut, to accommodate cutlery and utensils or spice bottles.

The result is a kitchen system that emphasizes effortless simplicity and functionality. A restricted range of materials has been used, without any obtrusive details. It is not stylistic mannerisms or formal gimmickry that give it an identity, instead the kitchen allows the architectural quality of the space in which it is installed to speak for itself. Volume, light and proportion are given due emphasis, rather than being upstaged by an object that constantly demands attention. Pawson's simplicity is an attempt to resolve the visual chaos of everyday life, to introduce a sense of order and calm. It does not deny the practical necessities, rather it provides an approach to accommodating them. His interiors do not eliminate possessions, but they are designed – usually with extensive ranges of white lacquered, polyester finish cupboard doors to hide every piece of domestic equipment – to eliminate their intrusiveness.

Pawson's design, just like his architecture, is unforced, but simplicity is not easily achieved. It is based on the idea of even the smallest things being done as well as possible, of excellence even in unseen details. The casual observer tends to see one Pawson design as flowing imperceptibly into the next. They certainly have things in common: the suppression of visual noise; the use of certain motifs, such as the 10 millimetre shadow gap in place of skirting that makes every wall appear to float. But they are each the product of specific circumstances. Ultimately, his work does not depend on the quality of the details, or on the ruthless consistency of finishes, but on the clear sight of the designer.

By the time that Pawson began to work with Obumex, he had designed a whole series of kitchens, both for his own use and for his clients. They used a variety of materials and approaches: some were freestanding objects within an interior; others were ranged

The stainless steel pivot hinges, designed to be invisible when the doors are closed, have the same precision as the more visible parts of the system.

against walls. Worktop materials included stainless steel, marble, and even a black resin composite used for acid resistant floors in power stations. The Obumex range was something else again. 'I never saw it as being based on my kitchen; it was starting again', says Pawson. Obumex had some well-defined ideas about what they wanted from Pawson, and gave him some parameters concerning the retail price and how many kitchens they would expect to make every year. But Pawson was more interested in getting right the fundamental idea of what a kitchen could be, than in setting out to meet the immediate targets. He simply looked at the basic elements that make up a kitchen. 'To me it always seemed that the worktop was the most important thing … a thin top would have been very thin, so that it would disappear altogether.' It was an option that had an appeal, but in the end Pawson opted for a unit with a thick top; the idea was to create a visual and functional distinction between the worktop and what went under it. The top would be designed to accommodate all the functional issues of a kitchen that involved liquids, cleaning, cutting, and also exposed hot plates. It would incorporate within it the sink, the waste disposal unit and the water outlet. Underneath would be the storage units and the domestic appliances. 'How you deal with what's under the worktop is almost as significant as the top. The front is important too, but if you make a hierarchy, it's the top you see first, and its from it that all the other decisions follow.'

As far as kitchen storage is concerned, there are two basic options; some people want open shelves, others want drawers. Pawson's approach is to offer both alternatives, and to combine them. For Obumex, the whole front of the units can be made to pull out, like a gigantic drawer. In fact, the whole point of the Obumex

system was to produce a kit of parts that could be used to create any form of kitchen. It can be free-standing or ranged against a wall, open or closed. The top can be any one of four very different materials; stainless steel, Carrara marble, lava stone or walnut. 'The kitchen can be anything the customer wants', says Pawson. 'It can be a block, or an island, which is when it looks its most beautiful, positioned in the middle of the room, with full-height cupboards behind – provided you have enough space.' For Pawson, steel is the preferred finish. 'It looks most effective when sink and the hob trim are all the same, it does away with one extraneous material, which makes it much simpler. It doesn't look like regular stainless steel, it has a reflective quality that makes it feel like something else altogether.'

The other major priority for Pawson was to design a kitchen that could subdue the visually chaotic jungle of consumerism that has overtaken kitchen appliances. Of course, all the necessary washing machines, dishwashers, ovens and refrigerators need to be accommodated within the system, but they should not be allowed to dominate their surroundings. 'I didn't want any visible reminders of brand names. If you install what are obviously Gaggenau appliances, then you are making a very clear statement about who you are. Likewise the Miele brand is an equally strong, but different statement.' To this end, the Obumex system is designed to wrap the necessary appliances; it visually subdues the kind of appliances that have actually been styled so that they will stand out in the shop against the competition, rather than look at home in the domestic setting.

But Pawson's Obumex kitchen doesn't stop at an elegant housing and a restrained, architectural aesthetic; he has added some special one-off elements to the system. The most distinctive visual element is the

The stainless steel work-
top appears to float above
the white laquered storage
units. The cast-steel controls, used to regulate both
the hobs and the water
supply, match the metal
finish of the worktop.

water spout, a stainless steel arc that is proportioned to reach both of a pair of sinks within a worktop. The taps are also specially made; fabricated rectangles of stainless steel, remote from the spout, and accommodated discreetly within the worktop. The taps use a vocabulary of form that is entirely different from the conventional language of taps, to suggest precision and quality. Even more discreet is the special overflow system for the sinks, a thin line representing the joint between the sink itself and the internal lining. Obumex also offers special square halogen hobs that Pawson designed for the system.

In one sense, Pawson's design is an exercise in control, in lifting the sense of oppression that comes from the clutter of things, and the visual chaos of superfluous complexity. It seeks to eliminate the distraction of awkward proportions and the constant irritation of the catch that does not function unobtrusively, or the tap that doesn't move smoothly and easily to deliver a finely judged quantity of water. In its place, he offers the comfort of exactness, of small things done well. Thus to Pawson, the way in which a cabinet meets a floor, or whether a door fits into a wall flush or proud, is not mere detail, but reflects fundamental questions.

When there is nothing to distract the eye, the thought that has gone into the positioning of a switch or a door, the curve of a spout against a slab of marble, the location of a chair, expand from being background into the foreground. When nothing is fudged, when every issue, even the smallest, is faced head on, and details are synthesized with space, then design can take on architectural qualities.

The double stainless steel sink is here accommodated within a stone version of the work-top. Water overflow is prevented by an invisible lip at the junction between stone and steel.

cathay pacific

The airport, along with the museum and the shopping mall, is one of the key public spaces that serve to define the contemporary city. An airport is a city gate, as well as being a national front door; it is a monument that celebrates the act of arrival and departure, and is an assertion of the nation state's prestige. It is a surrogate for the public realm, one that offers at least the illusion of a meeting place in which the rich and poor are in closer proximity than almost anywhere else in an increasingly economically segregated world.

Nor does the airport have just a purely symbolic role to play. It is an important bargaining counter in the economic competition between one city and another for trade and influence. There is an official, and an unofficial, side to the airport. Beneath the carefully burnished image of technocratic, but wholesome, modernity that creates a reassuringly secure atmosphere for the nervous traveller, there is a darker side. With their perpetually transient, anonymous population, airports are places in which crime of all kinds can flourish.

To accommodate such a complex and multi-layered environment, the airport has developed social hierarchies of public, private and semi-private spaces. There is the boundary set by customs and immigration officials that designates national from international territory. Even though they may overlap spatially, both sides have their own circulation routes, their own restaurants and shops, their own identity. There is the chaotic public world of the arrival and departure halls on the so called 'land side' of this boundary, where people congregate without needing to invest in the price of a ticket to gain access. The commercial world now fills such places with restaurants and supermarkets, and shops selling everything from Rolex watches to motorcars, and salami to soft toys; in some cases, even casinos and sex cinemas.

Behind the immigration security line, there is an even more tightly guarded boundary; the one that restricts access to the aircraft, defending them against the threat of terrorism and hijacking, as well as from the unwelcome attentions of smugglers. Thus, while an airport appears to be a public space, it is in fact experienced entirely differently by various groups of people as a series of separate private spaces.

In this hierarchy of space, the airlines have added yet another layer by offering their most valued customers the flattering illusion of access to at least part of the private world of the airport, away from the democratic scrum of the main halls. They offer a world guarded by a discreetly signalled door. Once you have passed through it, or even once you know of its existence, it becomes the sign of admission to an elite, a place in which to relax between and before flights, and in some cases, after them too. There is food, drink, something to read, a screen to watch and space to stretch out in. There are flowers, telephones, computers, desks and perhaps showers. All of these amenities are carefully graded according to the customer's importance to the airline, from the frequent flyer to the first-class passenger. Experienced from the subdued comfort of the lounge, and insulated from all the noise, the airport doesn't seem to be quite the same stressful madhouse as it can appear on the outside.

Hong Kong International Airport at Chek Lap Kok is built partly on reclaimed land. It replaces the territory's notorious Kai Tak, where the runway was so close to the city that descending jets appeared to skim the washing lines stretched between the surrounding high-rise apartment towers. Designed by Norman Foster, Chek Lap Kok is vast, covering as much land as a fair-sized European city. Its first runway is designed to

Part land reclaimed from the sea, part remodelled existing island, Hong Kong International Airport at Chek Lap Kok is one of Asia's most ambitious new construction projects. Norman Foster's terminal buildings are made up of a vaulted main departure hall, linked by a transit system to the most distant departure gates. The Cathay Lounge is on the left-hand side of the main terminal structure in the foreground.

overleaf The Wing has the scale of a building within a building. Foster's vaults sheltered the construction of the lounge, which depended on the craft skills of a range of specialists. It was prefabricated off site and shipped to Chek Lap Kok.

handle 35 million passengers a year, but later phases will more than double that capacity. Hong Kong is within five hours' flying time of half of the world's population, and it is determined to become the place where as many of those people as possible either catch, or more likely, change planes. But Singapore, Kuala Lumpur and Bangkok are all fighting to make themselves the primary hub for Asia. To this end, Hong Kong's outgoing colonial administration invested 19 billion American dollars in Chek Lap Kok, which involved building 34 kilometres of expressways and tunnels, a high-speed rail link, a brace of suspension bridges, to say nothing of a new town to accommodate airport staff. It took 20,000 workers to build it and the terminal sprawls over 464,000m^2. Inside its elegant glass and steel structure, global and local cultures are on a collision course. Foster's architecture has given Hong Kong a landmark of international significance. It is not its sheer size that makes Chek Lap Kok so impressive, it is the sense of order and calm that Foster has brought to the interior that makes it memorable. He has eliminated as much of the visual noise as possible, restricting the structure and the range of finishes to the minimum. At the same time, he has brought sunlight right into the heart of the building.

Inside this vast space you find almost all the elements of a contemporary city; offices, police stations, restaurants and bars. Despite Foster's urge for order, the chaotic quality of the contemporary Chinese city outside has managed to find its way into the very heart of the airport without diluting the strength of the original conception. Alongside two Harrods boutiques, and outlets for Cartier and Gucci, there is the Fook Ming Tong tea house, and a restaurant that seeks to evoke a back street dim sum bar from the Shanghai of the 1940s, complete with moongate and ancient bicycles.

Within the terminal building, Pawson's
lounge for Cathay Pacific was a deliberate attempt by
the Hong Kong-based airline to live up to the architecture of the new airport, as well as a commercial move
in the highly competitive travel market. On long-haul
flights to and from the Far East, there is almost always a
choice of route and airline connections, and by making
its lounge as distinctive as possible, Cathay is attempting to persuade passengers to choose to fly with them in
preference to other airlines. The lounge that passengers
encounter on the transit stop is a critical deciding factor
persuading them to opt for one route over another. It is
an extraordinary demonstration of the way that architecture can be used to warp space – a single room can have
the effect of altering the flow of traffic, diverting hundreds of thousands of people every year thousands of
miles across the globe. Cathay was aware that it had to
do something impressive at Chek Lap Kok to emphasize
that this was its home base. It had both a domestic and
an international audience to address. Peter Sutch,
Cathay's chairman, was clear that the airline wanted to
make a statement about itself and about Hong Kong.
'We wanted the lounge to compliment the architectural
setting of the airport, and we wanted to be different
from the competition.'

The airline had already been reinventing itself
for a post-colonial future even before Chek Lap Kok was
started. The Union Jack was removed from the hull of
Cathay's aircraft well before the colony's handover, and
its old livery was replaced with giant calligraphic brush
strokes, not actually Chinese characters, but designed
to suggest a non-specific Asian identity. 'We are not
about batik or Thai silk, we are the modern Asia. The fact
that we are not tied to a specific national identity, but
have a very strong home base in Hong Kong is actually a

plus in the Asian market.' The philosophy behind the look of the lounge revolved around the concept of 'modern Asia' – not specifically Chinese or Japanese, Korean or Thai, but a blend of all these cultures.

If the lounge had to look modern and Asian at the same time, it also had to convey the unmistakable imagery of luxury. Airlines market first class tickets that cost as much as the price of a family car with the promise that they bring with them the distillation of luxury and staff who minister to every whim.

The reality is that even first class passengers are crammed into an aluminium tube, with restricted leg room, for hours on end. On the ground, however, the lounge is the one place that offers the chance to make those passengers feel that they are special. Luxury, in the context of Hong Kong, is not an easy quality to get right. It is a place in which the big hotels routinely send chauffeur-driven Rolls Royce saloons to collect guests, and which has the details of luxury precisely worked out. To impress its jaded and demanding businessmen and women is no easy task.

The airline was working closely with the Hong Kong office of the Australian architectural practice Denton Corker Marshall on planning their airport buildings, and it was through them that Cathay began looking for a designer who could produce the kind of lounge that would make the statement they wanted. Pawson was invited to take part in the selection process, alongside a cross section of other architects from Britain and America. In the autumn of 1996, he found himself being interviewed in the offices of Cathay Pacific's parent company, the Swire Group, in a bland granite-faced high rise looking across Hong Kong harbour. This was a group whose natural style was deeply conservative. Luxury, as they saw it, was exemplified by the Mandarin

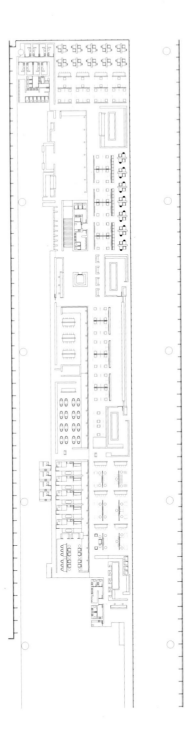

opposite The dark
granite stair propels the
passengers into the heart
of The Wing and offers
dramatic views of Foster's
great roof as they ascend.

left The Wing is mainly
accommodated in what
was originally intended to
be a mezzanine level viewing gallery in Foster's plan.
To the air side, The Wing
projects into the double-
height departure hall; on
the land side, it backs on
to the rear wall of Foster's
building. Service areas,
kitchens, lavatories and
stores are concentrated
here. The restaurants,
cabanas, library – all the
quieter areas – are located
in a strip of accommo-
dation at the side of the
mezzanine, while the
more sociable seating
and work areas look
towards the runways.

Cathay's passengers can
look out over the etched-
glass screen into the
double-height departure
hall, but cannot them-
selves be seen from below.

previous page The Wing
offers a variety of spaces
with very different qual-
ities. The business class
library reading room is a
place in which to sit and
relax. Natural light filters
through the etched glass
screen on the left, catching
the gentle ripples on the
surface of the pool that
runs its entire length.

Oriental Hotel, measured by conspicuously lush materials; comfort levels are signalled by the depth of the cushions and the elaborate carpets.

Swire is one of Hong Kong's more remarkable institutions, a trading house established soon after the colony was created, run with more than a passing resemblance to a feudal fiefdom. It is dominated by succeeding generations of the original founding family, and managed by a small cadre of so called 'house' staff, recruited every year from Britain, mainly from the older universities. It is their role to oversee local employees and maintain the Swire ethos, much like a commercial version of a colonial civil service.

Pawson's original presentation was thorough. He brought a powerful collection of images and words that captured the stress and chaos of the contemporary city, and contrasted it with the oasis of calm and quiet that he was proposing to create at the airport. This message, and the serious effort and commitment that Pawson had clearly put into the proposal, certainly impressed Cathay. He was hired and found himself working on a commission that was far larger in its extent than anything he had attempted before. Not only that, but it meant working for a very different kind of client from those that he was used to. Cathay is not a personality-driven business, like Calvin Klein's, in which one individual takes responsibility for every decision. It is run by a hierarchy of committees reporting to a board, with shareholders to consider. The lounge was a commission that revolved around image, but also had to deal with a tough deadline that could not be ducked, and the preconceptions of a much wider range of customers than a fashion store or an art gallery.

The airport in Hong Kong was going to open in 1998, come what may; Cathay simply had to have its

previous page Etched glass screens do not disrupt the open quality of the space, but break up the impact of the sheer scale and size of the first-class lounge and help to define sheltered areas within it.

lounge ready to deal with that. The space would have to be tough enough to deal with the punishment of the heavy use meted out by millions of passengers each year. It would also be subjected to the highly critical eyes of these same passengers with all their expectations of what constituted luxury and comfort, and what did not.

To complicate matters, Hong Kong was in the midst of the preparation for the handover of the colony back to China. Beijing had initially been suspicious of the entire airport project. Even when China was convinced, the airport authority team building the project realized that they would, one day, have a Chinese management to answer to.

The space allocated to Cathay had been a public viewing gallery in Foster's original scheme. The airport authority saw renting it out to an airline as a strictly commercial proposition. Cathay was the only tenant likely to need enough square footage to fill all of it, yet the authority drove a hard bargain all the same, setting the rental at levels comparable to those in Hong Kong's central business district. Even extracting the plans took considerable effort before Pawson could start work on designing the lounges within the space in detail. Pawson's intention was that the lounge, or the 'The Wing' as Cathay call it, would not intrude into Foster's concept of the space, nor would it involve alterations to the exterior of the terminal.

The commission from Cathay to design The Wing represented a challenge. 'This is something new for me. It's the first time I've done something which is not based only on a palette of white walls. It has to work in the demanding context of an airport and yet retain the essence of simplicity. I've always seen the project not simply as an interior, but as a building within a building, a piece of architecture in its own right.'

So, what can an airline offer to make the experience of travel a more civilized one, on the ground as well as in the air? For Pawson the solution was to find ways to give its most regular passengers the chance to find a place where they can feel that they are on their own turf rather than on somebody else's. The further you are away from home in the impersonal, anonymous world of air travel, the more precious is the rare experience of finding an enclave which feels like part of your own domestic life.

The Wing is conceived and planned as an environment which relates to, and is part of, the airport as a whole. It is not a sealed box, nor is it hidden away down a warren of endless corridors and harsh neon. Pawson's design is based on the idea of bringing natural light into, what is conventionally treated as, the hermetic world of an airport. It offers space, quietness, a chance to decompress from the stress of the city and the pressure of the aircraft. The project is based on an architectural language that is subtle and delicate, a strategy that is in itself unusual in the context of an airport, where blandness is the usual alternative to brashness. Pawson offers the magical effect of light on water, gently rippling on the surface of the pool that runs the entire length of The Wing, seen through the etched glass that divides enclosed spaces from the open part of the lounge.

The areas for first class and business class are grouped together, arranged back to back, but each has its own entrance. First class passengers come in on the upper level of the terrace which houses the lounge, as soon as they have gone past the immigration controls. Business class passengers have a slightly less direct route, beyond immigration controls and a little way into the gate area before turning left and up into their lounge

Most airline lounges are introverted spaces. Cathay's wing has private areas, but it also has the Long Bar, with its stainless steel top and specially made, leather-topped stools, which offers a spectacular view out over the main runway and the mountains beyond.

opposite In this computer rendering, the first class dining room with its Danish furniture, and the pool, has the style and atmosphere of a formal restaurant.

area. Throughout the lounge, Pawson uses a dark, monumental stone, which provides a powerful and effective contrast to the lightness and fragility of Foster's delicate steel roof. There is a creative tension between the two, almost as if a classicist had built a pavilion under the soaring vaults of a Gothic cathedral.

The majority of the accommodation is on the upper level, a mezzanine that runs the length of the departure hall. The effect is like the main deck of an ocean liner. Cathay's passengers can look out over the rail of their deck, down on the main passenger waiting area, and across to the spectacular view of mountains, ocean and descending jets coming in to land. Pawson's plan grouped eating and relaxing spaces behind a wall that runs the whole length of The Wing. The outer side is open to the terminal building, and looks out over the public areas. Inside, behind an etched glass wall and a water pool, are the more private areas. Peter Sutch says 'We stayed away from gimmicks, there are no golf driving ranges, we are more serious than that.' Pawson came up with a list of things that he saw as relaxing and luxurious. He proposed private baths for first class passengers, a restaurant offering food as good as any restaurant in the world, a library stocked with fine art books, and a long bar serving cocktails. Each passenger would also have their own work space.

Most of Cathay's long-haul flights leave late in the evening, so The Wing is designed to enable passengers to do a full day's work, then drive directly out to the airport where they can enjoy a relaxed dinner, watch a video or television, even take a relaxing bath before they get on the aircraft and go straight to sleep, rather than wait until 1am for dinner.

Cathay were committed to the concept, but as the project continued, the management team

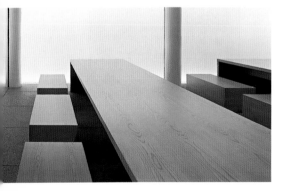

Sheltered by translucent glass walls from the outer bar area, business class passengers can relax in a café that offers long refectory-style tables and douglas fir benches. The floor is made of the same hammered granite as the rest of the lounge.

became increasingly anxious about whether their customers would understand the design. The airline's rhetoric was modern Asia, with which Pawson's austere simplicity fits perfectly in theory. But in practice, modern Asia is populated by more label-conscious Chinese businessmen and women with a fondness for ancient brandies that come in boxes lined in crushed velvet, than it is by travelling art directors in Yohji Yamamoto black linen suits.

The airline requested a full-size mock up to assess the impact of Pawson's design, in particular of the furniture then being manufactured in Italy to his specifications. Would it be comfortable enough? Would the business class restaurant, with its refectory tables, remind the passengers, as it did some of the Cathay management, of their school canteen? And why was Pawson refusing to put down a carpet?

A spare parts shed on the airline's engineering base at Kai Tak was allocated for the purpose. Prototype versions of the tables and chairs were shipped out, but the scale of the interior was missing; so was the lighting, the view and the water. In the Cathay maintenance base, a 5-metre long table was crammed into a 6-metre long room, with a ceiling just 2.4 metres high. The Swire management wandered in, their arms folded, kicking things as if they were buying second hand cars. 'All they could say was that it looked monumental' recalls Pawson. The specially chosen colour of the leather on the sofas suggested mud to the Cathay team, rather than the exquisite cigar leaf colour that Pawson had in mind; he was disconcerted. In his terms, The Wing was already too busy and too full of incident, and yet it didn't satisfy his clients. 'I was offering them what I thought was a huge compromise, and they said, "We must have comfort, we must have colour".'

Then, instead of inviting celebrated European restaurants to take on the catering, the airline opted for the food and beverage department of the Peninsula Hotel, an operation that inevitably would put the pragmatism of portion control ahead of the brio of a more individualistic operation. Unlike Kai Tak, which had a night flights curfew to keep noise levels acceptable, Chek Lap Kok can operate round the clock. And, when flights are disrupted or delayed, The Wing may not close for days. In routine operation, it is constantly in use from 6am to 1am. It has to be kept immaculate and present food that is appetizing, and looks good, day and night.

Cathay knew that they didn't want a lounge that looked conventional. According to Sutch, 'It had to look exceptionally different, a new airport was a once in a lifetime chance to do something special.' Pawson's response was to maintain the basic plan, but to soften the interior with a selection of the most beautiful pieces of furniture that he could find. He chose modern classics that were unusual enough not to have been reduced to the status of visual clichés. He looked at Denmark and Kaare Klint, at Austria and Josef Hoffmann. He introduced a few silk and wool rugs on parts of the floor.

The result is an interior of a refinement that is rarely achieved in an airport. It is the only part of the interior of Chek Lap Kok in which a designer has responded to the quality of Foster's building, co-opting the soaring roof, and used a palette of carefully chosen materials – stone, timber, glass and steel – that has a logic of its own, yet responds to, rather than fights with, the rest of the terminal. It is an assertion of the possibility of a civilizing space within what is, conventionally, a de-personalized environment.

As the passenger arrives at The Wing, a flight of grey granite steps propels them skyward, offering a

To decompress from the tension of a long-haul flight, or to relax after a day's work before catching a late departure, Cathay's first class passengers can make use of individual cabanas, each with a bath and terrace. Each cabana is screened from view by acid-etched glass. The semi-private terrace has a lounger looking over the pool running the length of the lounge. Beyond is the translucent wall forming the outer edge of the private areas of The Wing.

glimpse of Foster's great roof, into the heart of The Wing, which is another powerful space defined by a series of granite pylons. One houses the lift, another contains the reception desk on the upper level, yet another accommodates magazine and newspaper displays. Together they create a craggy, stepped outline etched in profile against the background of the soaring roof.

The terminal building provides the landscape setting on which The Wing sits. In effect, The Wing is a string of one- and two-storey buildings anchored to a series of patios and terraces. The terminal and The Wing represent two clearly different aesthetic approaches to architecture. Foster's patient engineering skill has succeeded in turning steel components into industrial jewellery. Pawson's sensual pleasure in space, in particular the transition from one volume to another, and his refined use of materials heighten tactile awareness of the surroundings. The two approaches conduct a gentle dialogue.

The full extent of the lounges is not immediately apparent. The point is not only to avoid creating the impression that this is a giant barn; Pawson has also created a series of different spaces without any sense of forced novelty or artificial incident. One area leads naturally into the next. Some are enclosed, such as the business class library and the café; others are more open and fluid. The long bar is aligned along the edge of the balcony, its teams of barmen working with their backs to the view. The patrons look over their heads towards the runway and the sea, a low partition separating them from the clusters of comfortable, leather armchairs.

Running through the centre of the lounge, cleverly screened by partitions, is a strip of water. Gently agitated by a mechanical pump, it can be glimpsed from the outside in the form of ripples of light unfolding over the outer face of the etched partition panels. Inside, it defines the edge of the succession of interior spaces. It courses through the first class library, where the tones of brown leather and rich timber are set off by the white walls and granite floor. Then there is the succession of bath cabanas in first class, equipped with a little internal terrace along which the pool laps gently. The stream then unwinds through the first class restaurant, moving finally through the business class library. Each of these spaces has a different quality and yet they are designed in a way which clearly relates one to another. Pawson's palette of tones and materials is exceptionally refined and delicate, running in a range of infinitely subtle gradations from the pale granite of the floor to the quiet glow which suffuses the partition walls, and the more luminous glow of the specially designed screens within the seating area, where glass sandwiches a specially made internally lit Japanese paper.

Within The Wing, a white wall which is punctured by distracting banks of light switches or marred by a door in a visually uncomfortable position does not register on the senses in the same way as a plain white wall. It is on the clutter that the eye focuses; and the Cathay Wing is about removing clutter. There are places to be sociable, places where the bustle of travel may be enjoyed and a variety of spaces in which to withdraw from it. It is an essential part of Pawson's architectural philosophy that creating calm ordered spaces depends on concentrating on the essentials.

young vic

In its present form, the Young Vic Theatre was first conceived in 1968, and as such it belongs to the golden age of cultural radicalism in Britain. It grew out of one of London's most famous theatres, the Old Vic, the temporary base of the National Theatre Company in the 1960s, while its monumental, purpose-designed complex was being built nearby overlooking the Thames.

While they were at the Old Vic, Laurence Olivier, Frank Dunlop and others set up a programme of performances by younger actors, aimed at young audiences. It was such a success that a group of directors and actors around the company decided to give it an independent existence and a home of its own. The existing Young Vic Theatre was built as a cultural experiment, with Arts Council support, more than a quarter of a century ago. It was a deliberate attempt to bring theatre out of the West End, to involve young people and to try to build a new audience for theatre. It set out to be accessible in its repertoire and pricing policy, but also in the way that it looked, and its location. Situated in what was then the cheerfully run-down hinterland of Waterloo Station, it was surrounded by street markets and council houses.

Money was tight, so rather than create a polished piece of architecture, the building was always envisaged as being temporary – it would be better to build something that would not last, than nothing at all. Bill Howell, a partner in the practice of Howell Killick Partridge and Amis, designed a building that was planned to last no more than five years. He used the most economical of materials: concrete, blockwork and the plainest finishes. The new theatre co-opted the remains of the existing buildings that had stood on the site.

The main foyer space was created out of an old butcher's shop front. There was no attempt to prettify or conceal the simple structure, which was braced externally by exposed steel rods, like a gasometer. Where two skins of blockwork met, the edge was left rough and unfinished.

Now that all theatres put accessibility as a priority, it is hard to remember just how radical the Young Vic seemed when it was first opened, and how much it has done to change the nature of theatre in Britain. Drawing on the experience of the Edinburgh Festival Theatre, Howell's design ignored the proscenium arches of the eighteenth and nineteenth centuries and returned to an amphitheatre arrangement, an open arena that recalls the classical and Elizabethan theatres in the round. It was done not as a reference to the past, but to create a more dramatic setting for theatre. In conventional Victorian theatres, the audience was segregated into separate tiers that were each decorated and equipped to reflect the price that their patrons were paying, and they were confronted head on by a stage; their experience of the play was shaped mainly by the sight of rows and rows of intervening heads. The Young Vic, by contrast, was self-consciously egalitarian. The audience shared the same entrance, paid the same low ticket price and enjoyed an equally good view of the stage. Moreover, because the theatre took the form of an arena, they had the sense of an intense, shared experience, aware of themselves occupying the space alongside the cast, and of more spectators beyond the stage.

As it was originally built, the Young Vic had just one stage and the main auditorium, which seats up to 500 people. In the 1980s, what had been the old rehearsal space was converted into a studio theatre with room for about 100. Audiences found themselves expected to sit on puritanical benches instead of plush seats; there were no carpets or chandeliers. But while all this was part of the conventional rhetoric of the time, the

The Young Vic's original
building, designed by Bill
Howell, was never intended
to be permanent. The
exposed steel structure,
the simple blockwork and
the auditorium had an aesthetic bluntness that made
a virtue out of necessity.
The success of the compa-
ny, however, has made the
creation of a new theatre
essential.

theatre has proved a real success, with a character of its own that has allowed it to outlive the passing fads of theatrical fashion.

'The Young Vic has an extraordinary balance between the actor and the audience', says well-known theatre director, Adrian Noble. 'It's not a theatre that forces the play to take one particular line or another: it's a harmonious space.' Some of what have turned out to be Britain's most successful actors and directors began their careers in this theatre, and it has been a place in which many of the theatre's most established stars have been happy to work.

In the nature of things, a building that has been designed for a strictly limited life span always begins to wear out. It is possible to repaint the interior every so often, but leaks and the lack of air conditioning are not so easily remedied. Nor is a layout which simply cannot accommodate wheelchairs in the auditorium, or even in the box office, subject to straightforward solutions. Even the functional performance of the theatre is not what it was. The evolution of the Young Vic's range of activities has meant that the theatre now needs more space for performance, rehearsals and to carry out its educational role.

After the establishment of the Arts Council's lottery fund in 1995, which aimed to channel money into the fabric of both new and existing arts buildings, the Young Vic began to consider its options. To do nothing was not a defensible strategy; sooner or later it would be impossible to go on using the building as it stood. Everything needed upgrading and improving, from the sound and lighting equipment to the creation of a full thrust stage. A ventilation and air-conditioning system needed to be installed. The backstage areas needed renovation. There was no satisfactory permanent, yet

flexible, seating structure. The foyer hardly existed and the public toilets were worn out. There was an existing bar and restaurant area, but properly developed it could make a lot more income for the Young Vic. There was no space for a rehearsal room, which meant that money was wasted on hiring space off site. There was no teaching space, storage areas or a set construction workshop and scene dock. The company looked at other sites, but there was nothing suitable nearby, and so, despite the qualities of the building, they decided to opt for demolishing the original structure and starting again. It was the only viable long term alternative.

The approach that Pawson was encouraged to pursue in rebuilding the Young Vic, was to recreate its essential qualities, while overcoming the shortcomings of its original budget. After a competitive interview, he was appointed to steer the scheme through a feasibility study, and to make a lottery application having designed the new theatre. It was a commission that asked him to explore new territory. Before the Waddington Gallery, Pawson had been closely involved in the contemporary art world, but he had little experience of the theatre. As Pawson saw it, this was not necessarily a disadvantage. 'Perhaps with the gallery, a little learning can be a dangerous thing. You think that you know more than you really do. This way, I spend a lot of time listening to people who work in the theatre and looking at what they think are successful theatres … But of course, you don't have to be an actor to design a theatre.'

Pawson approached the theatre without the preconceptions that a specialist might have done. 'I am happy to accept a classical shape, I don't have any preconceptions about, for example, having to have a flat roof as an overriding objective. There are certain laws in theatres, and they can tell you the basics to get right. But

opposite Pawson's design for the theatre takes as its starting point the special qualities of the original auditorium, in particular its intimacy and its flexibility. Various different seating models were investigated to recapture those qualities for the new building.

below Cross section through the auditorium. The new theatre would be built to the edges of the site to maximize usable space.

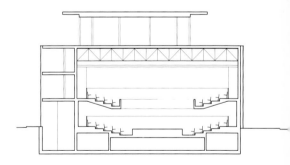

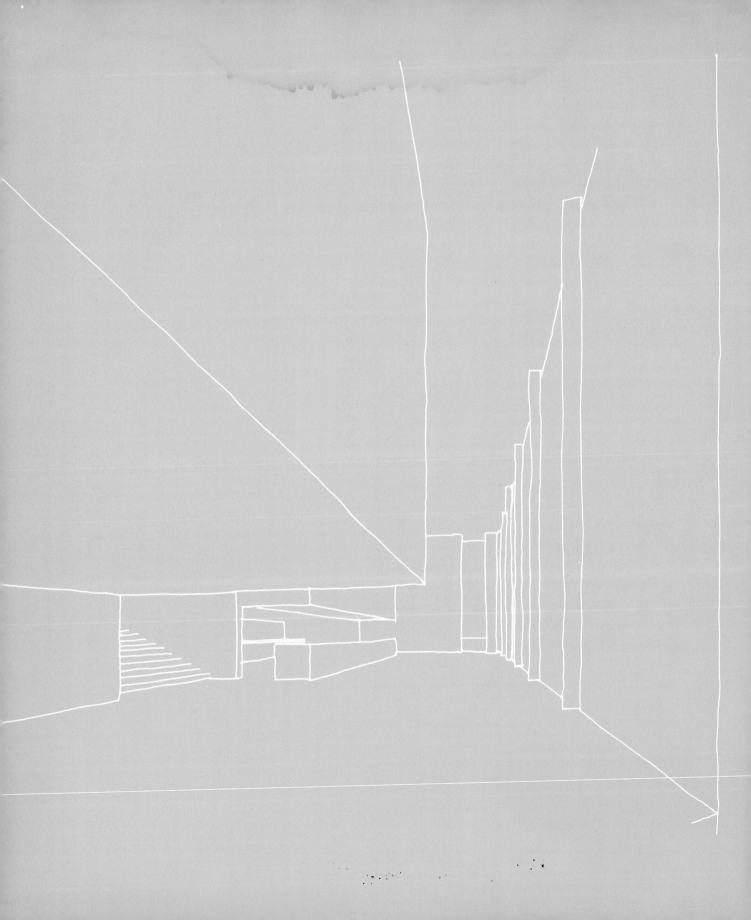

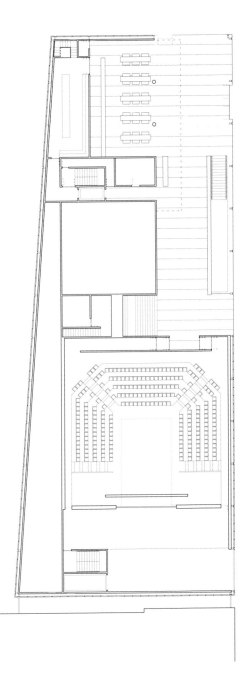

The elements of the
theatre, main auditorium
and studio theatre read as
discrete forms within an
overall envelope.

The foyer is shaped by
the major volumes of the
theatre to accommodate
the new box office, the
restaurant and the bar.

opposite Longitudinal
section through the lobby.
Pawson's new buildings
give the Young Vic the
front of house facilities it
has always lacked.

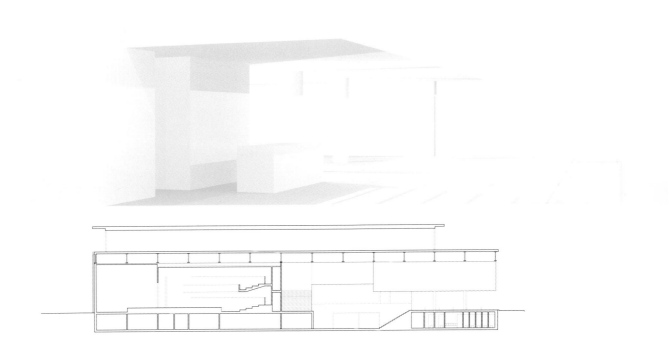

they can't tell you the magic ingredient for a beautiful atmosphere in a theatre. It's like designing a church. The rules can tell you what you need in practical terms, but not the things that will make it sacred.'

The original auditorium was conceived as an intimate thrust stage. It was an exceptionally innovative and influential design for 1968, and today, despite its limitations, it is still one of the most adaptable auditoria in London and is much sought after for its unique intimacy. However, initial design limitations mean that a degree of inflexibility remains, ensuring that it will never achieve its full potential. The configuration of the stage restricts the building of thrust stages to the back wall at floor level, forcing them to be at least 1.2 metres off the ground. The company want the new auditorium to replicate the intimacy of this original, with its ideal size, as the centrepiece of the new theatre; but they want it to be more flexible. In the end, the solution adopted was to design a thrust stage capable of being turned into a theatre-in-the-round.

The theatre as it stands occupies a rectangular peninsula site, bounded by streets on three sides, although one of them is a tightly restricted alley, and overlooked by blocks of flats. To accommodate all the extra space that is needed, implies a footprint that goes right to the edge of the building line, and rises to three storeys. It is this envelope that Pawson has adopted as the starting point for his scheme. Within it, there are three clearly differentiated volumes: the main auditorium, the studio theatre space and the teaching space. The main auditorium is moved towards the western boundary of the site and the studio theatre is located immediately to its east. The teaching space is on the other side of the main auditorium. The space left over creates, at the front, a public foyer, bar and restaurant and, to the rear, the scene dock and workshop space that services the three volumes. Backstage access is taken to the west of the main auditorium from Cons Street, which allows lorries to be unloaded indoors, and reduces disturbance to local residents.

The building is also given a skin, partly made up of timber slats, partly of translucent glass. 'The relationship between solid and transparent is the key to the exterior. It looks like two cubes touching each other. The idea was to find a glass that was translucent, but with an opaque quality. That would mean in the day time, you don't see out, because the view is not that good, but at night passers by could see in.' The timber slats, cladding the full height of segments of the exterior, would be a major aesthetic element. Pawson is looking for a local reference in the area to guide the final choice of which timber to use. 'It needs to be able to weather well, and soften the exterior.'

Designing a theatre does represent a conflict. 'There is a lot of psychology to get right. I prefer not to have a balcony, because that breaks up what you are looking at. And big, empty walls don't warm up an audience. You need to be able to see other people from wherever you sit in the theatre, it's what makes the place come alive; the audience actually warm themselves up.'

The main auditorium is an update of the straightforward quality of the original, but it will last longer and reflect a richer palette. Specially designed oak benches, pierced with rectangular openings like ship's decking, will give a sense of warmth. This interior relies more on the people in it, than on the spatial purity which is normally the basis of Pawson's architecture. He sees the auditorium as going back to first principles. 'We want to go back to Epidaurus, with comfortable seats.'

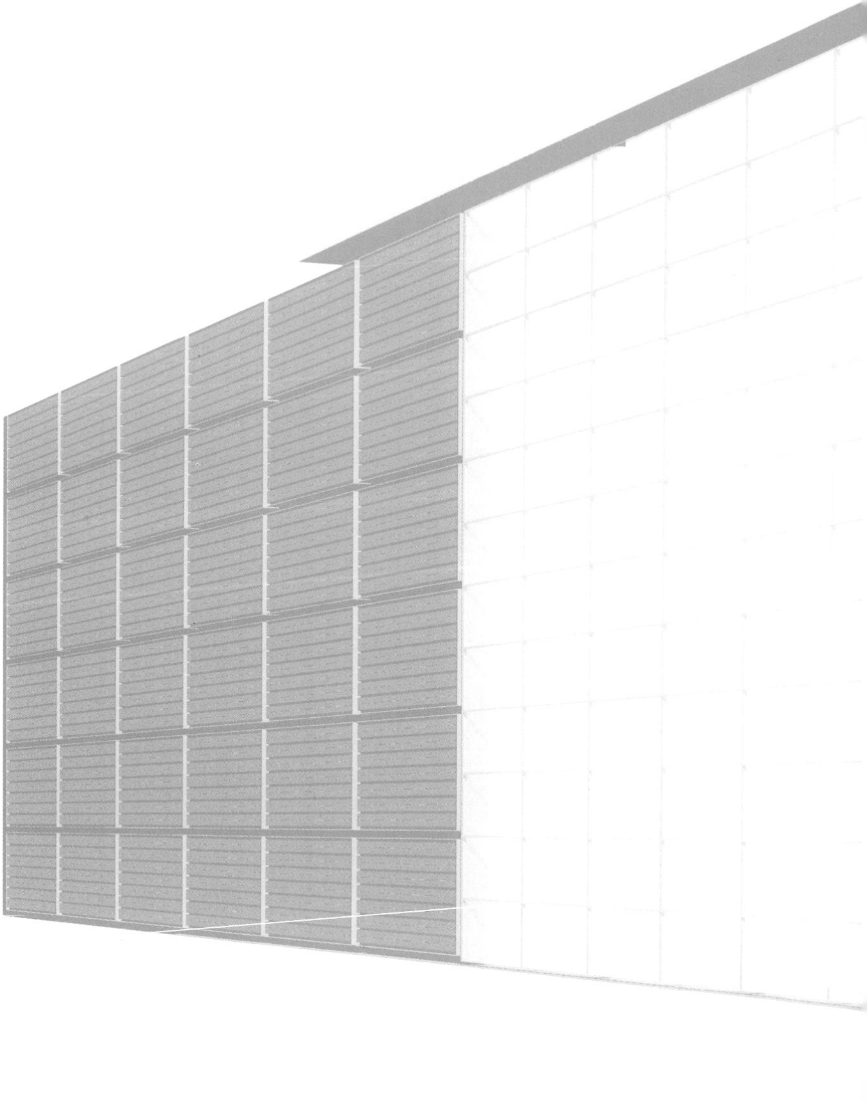

The glass facade facing
the street is intended to
make the building seem
welcoming both day and
night. Varying degrees
of transparency will ensure
that the theatre foyer has
an appropriate degree
of privacy.

stewart house

There is a ten-minute wait for the car ferry for the short trip over to Long Island's South Fork. It is the invisible line between two different Americas. Behind is Shelter Island, a world of boat sheds, wharves and ancient rusting sedans parked with the keys left in the ignition. Ahead lies East Hampton; the most glossily well-scrubbed, affluent zip code east of Beverley Hills. In the summer, its streets are crammed with the rich and famous, darting from the Barefoot Contessa's gourmet sandwich counter, to the Ralph Lauren store, to the American Civil Liberties Union fundraiser. The radio abruptly stops playing the thoughtful, well-bred chamber music that is the hallmark of American public broadcasting stations. 'And now this message. "Hi, I'm Martha Stewart, and I'm here to talk about fish".'

Martha Stewart is a phenomenon. She used the catering business that she started as a means of asserting her independence from her publisher ex-husband, as the launchpad for a career that has established her as America's most unassailable, and most profitable, taste-maker; a Terence Conran and a Delia Smith rolled into one. There is a magazine that bears her name and sells hundreds of thousands of copies every month, full of her helpful suggestions on table decorations and kitchen layouts; a syndicated television programme that brings the process to live-action life; a publishing company that turns out books full of recipes and tips on entertaining with style. There is a licensing arm producing, among much else, tins of Martha Stewart paint. The ethos is not just about how to do it; Stewart is offering a vision of how to live, a powerful mix of Victorian self-improvement with contemporary style. It has been a very successful formula. In the summer of 1999, Stewart took the company public with a floatation on the New York stock exchange. It is a move that has had an exceptionally good press from the financial analysts: 'A well focused business, run by an intelligent Chief Executive Officer who knows what she is doing, unlike so many of the internet-related offerings that are cluttering up the new issues market', said the *New York Observer*. The market agreed, shares tripled in value within hours. Stewart is high profile enough to have spawned a flourishing parody industry, fuelled by those who are amused by what they see as her presumption in prescribing a way of life for the rest of us. And now here she is, in disembodied voice if not quite in person, telling us how to prod the flesh of sea bass to check how fresh it is, and how to use lime to add zest to its flavour.

The house that she has been working on for herself for almost five years is positioned at the epicentre of the Hamptons, right on Georgica Pond. Georgica is an inlet, cut off from the open Atlantic by a sand bar, where the houses are made all but invisible by thick stands of trees. This is where Hillary and Bill Clinton spend at least part of their summers, and where Steven Spielberg moved when the riots and the forest fires of Los Angeles finally became too much. Richard Meier and Calvin Klein both have houses nearby. The core of East Hampton is still intact; its clapboard puritan churches and its windmills that date back to the 1640s are within an easy walk of Georgica – even though nobody would dream of walking. In the distance are the town beaches, where white sands merge imperceptibly into the spray and the cornflower blue horizon. The old potato fields have vanished, subdivided to create plots for huge houses hidden behind solid walls of hedges that are maintained immaculately by armies of operatives, who descend on the winding roads of the area once a week. They come to cut, trim and clean up, doing their best not to get in the way of the similarly equipped

overleaf The rectangular Bunshaft House, which now belongs to Martha Stewart, is positioned to the right of the point that juts into the pond.

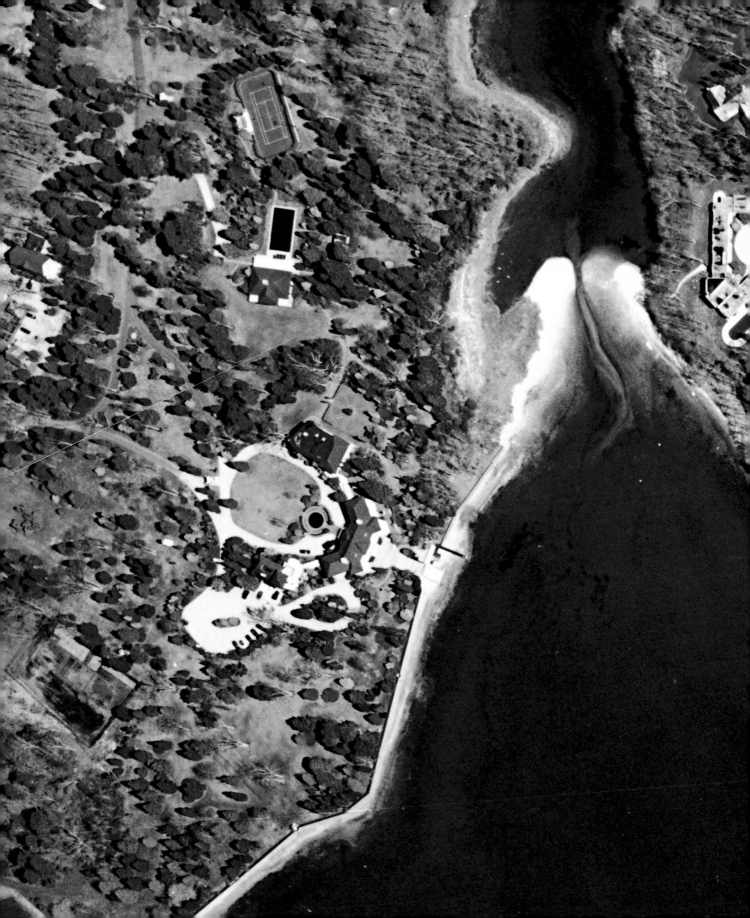

The house was built by
Gordon Bunshaft in 1963
for himself and his wife,
Nina. The siting is masterly,
set well back from the
waterfront, so as to make
the most of the remarkable
view and, at the same time,
to avoid intruding on the
beauty of the setting.

opposite The external skin
of what is now the Stewart
house has been untouched,
but the interior has been
scooped out, in order to be
completely remodelled.

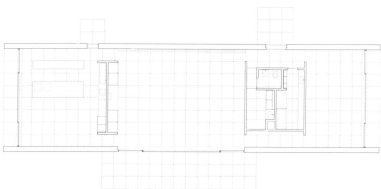

teams working the same circuit to deal with the pools, to say nothing of the armies of caterers, florists, cleaners, tennis coaches and cooks on whom every East Hampton summer depends.

East Hampton is the complete antithesis of the other end of Long Island, just two hours away, where the edges of New York City crumble into dereliction and squalor. Here, you find a hyper real, exaggerated version of the American good life, in which every corner is scrubbed and tended. The old beach houses made from wind-bleached timber – in which New York's literate middle classes once spent their summers sheltering behind insect screens and lounging on the wraparound porch – are giving way to the cult of gigantism that is overtaking every aspect of America. Every house here now has a guest house. Every guest house and every garage has its own subsidiary guest house. Every pool has a pool house. Every drive has never less than three recreational vehicles, barely house-trained pick-up trucks, pumped up on steroids so that they require a step ladder just to reach the running board. The houses themselves start with a minimum of 5,000 square feet, to accommodate all those restaurant standard professional kitchens, dens, computer rooms, guest bedrooms, pantries, wine cellars, games rooms and libraries that even the smallest nuclear families believe they can't do without. This is where the bull market of the last five years has really made its mark, transforming the domestic landscape to make way for the newly affluent. The style of choice of these masters of the universe runs from New England hacienda to Versailles provençal. Venture round the roads that fringe Georgica Pond and you will sense, rather than see, the changes that have taken place. The new houses are built expressly to make as much out of the view as possible, which means not only can you not

Pawson's additions consist of a pool with ancillary accommodation and a garage. The original house and the square block of the studio retain their relationship with the water and are positioned away from the road.

The pool is aligned parallel to the house, and connected to it with a carefully organized network of paths. It is set away from the water's edge and screened from the road by trees and the ancillary changing rooms.

previous page and below
The pool is anchored
within the landscape and
given an architectural
coherence by its relationship with three cabana
changing rooms aligned
along one edge.

opposite The garage,
pool and cabanas under
construction. The new
accommodation is con-
fined to the land side of
the existing house, with
pool huts organized around
the pool.

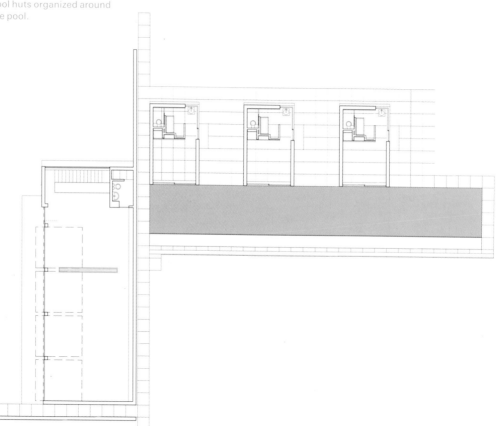

see them, but you can't see the water either. The street side planting blocks the view of the house; and even if you could see through the hedge, the house blocks the view of the water beyond. You will, however, become all too aware of the distant presence of Ron Perleman, owner of the Revlon empire, and his very ample water-side house. Venture too close to his driveway and armed guards will politely see you off the property.

In the midst of this solid wall of well-mani-cured, conspicuous consumption, there is one gap in the lush green privet. It marks the entrance to the house that Gordon Bunshaft built for himself back in 1963 when this was still haute Bohemia, and which Stewart acquired after his death in 1994. The driveway is blocked by a chainlink fence strung between galvanized steel posts. At the entrance, there are three official building permits, carrying serious looking stamps, lashed to what look like totem poles. Beyond the fence, rusting strands of reinforcing steel sprout from the weeds, and neatly dug trenches bear witness to a building project that has slowed down to a prolonged pause. The con-tractor has carefully tidied up the site, moved his equip-ment and trucks away, to await further instructions.

Bunshaft was one of the leading American architects of his generation. He ran the New York office of Skidmore Owings & Merrill at the time when it was the largest practice in the world. He helped to set the agenda for dignified, mainstream modern architecture for two or more decades. The firm built high-rise office towers, banks, embassies and airports all around the world. In New York, the firm gave some of the key stretches of Park Avenue and Avenue of the Americas their identity in the 1950s. It was an architecture that was based on a commercialized version of the Modern Movement, in particular as it was interpreted by Mies van der Rohe.

Bunshaft's house, designed for himself and his wife, Nina, embodies the spirit of his approach. It was, of course, on an entirely different scale from the usual output of the office but, with its travertine-faced concrete box structure, entirely windowless on the street side, it is clearly rooted in the same aesthetic, and it serves to remind us why the architecture of the 1960s used to be viewed with such suspicion. By the time Bunshaft died, his architecture was out of fashion, identified with all the grimmest, brutalist concrete boxes of the period. For Martha Stewart to buy such a house at all is a reflection of the renewed interest that America is now taking in its recent past. It is also evidence of the way that her own tastes have begun to embrace the contemporary; a suggestion of an imminent shift in wider popular taste that is still to come. But what attracted her most was the unique natural setting that the house enjoys.

Bunshaft sited his house with masterly discretion. He set it well back from the waterfront, so as to make the most of the remarkable view and, at the same time, to avoid intruding on the beauty of the setting. It is right at the commanding point of the pond, directly opposite the opening to the ocean, as if it were at the centre of the dress circle. The main house is positioned at an oblique angle across the site. You get no inkling of the presence of the water as you approach the house on foot; there is no advance warning of the view. Even when you enter through the single door at the back, the house still doesn't give up its secrets all at once. You find a screen wall, and it is only once you have negotiated it that the house finally reveals the view, which is the whole point of its existence. Whatever the eventual verdict of the history of the architecture of the house, its siting within the landscape is exemplary.

Bunshaft's original conception for the house, with its travertine-faced walls and the distinctive precast concrete clerestories, remains uncompromised, but Pawson's remodelling of the interior and upgrading of the finishes will give it a new quality and character.

overleaf The new pool, cabanas and garage take their geometry from the original buildings and enter into a spatial dialogue with them. The new work is conceived as a set of variations on Bunshaft's original theme; taking its lead from what is already there, while also bringing to it an architectural repertoire that is itself rooted in a sense of continuity and timelessness.

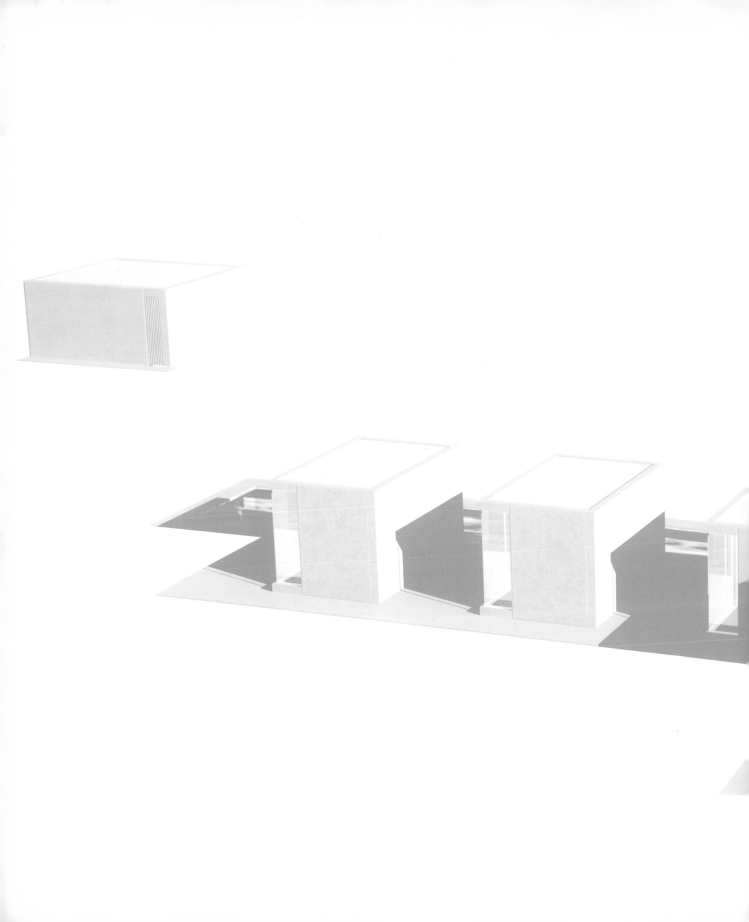

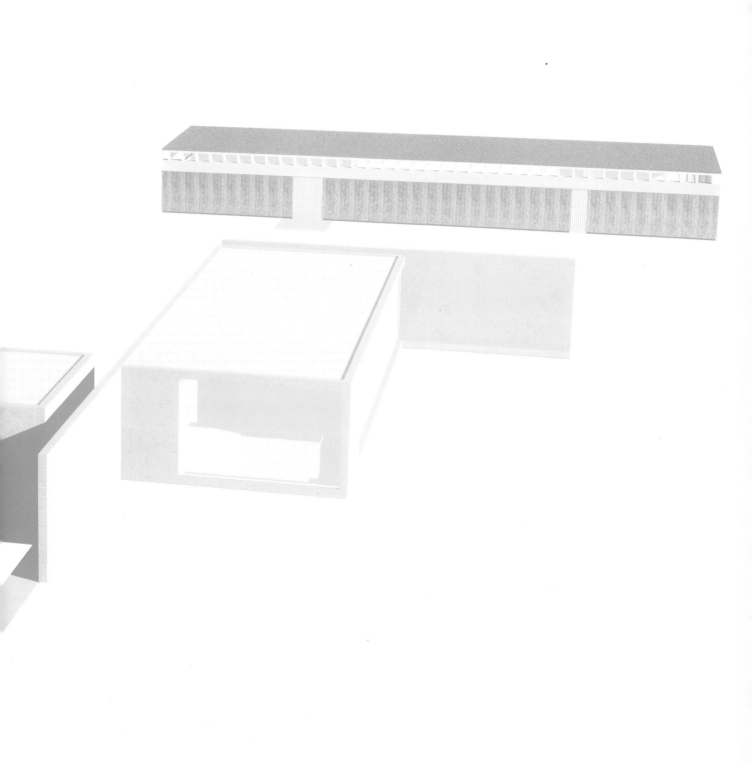

If the house is beautifully and intelligently located, its original internal arrangements left something to be desired. The kitchen, for example, was very much a perfunctory adjunct to the main space, shut off from it and with no view of the water. The interior was dominated by the roof, made up of uncompromising precast, U-shaped structural channels; even in 1963, this was an architecture that was no longer fashionable. There is a secondary building on the site which had been used as a studio by Bunshaft's wife. It has a timber-framed structure, but with its white painted wood and dark tinted glass, it is visually indistinguishable from the main house. By today's standards in the Hamptons, it was modest to the point of representing privation.

Modernization would necessarily involve much more than redecoration and rewiring; at the very least it would mean building a pool and a garage. When Stewart bought the house, it was clear from the start that it was too important an icon of American Modernism for total demolition to be an option. It was also situated on a delicate piece of coastal ecology, so only the lightest-of-touch development was permissible, despite the excesses being built all around. It was also surrounded by homes belonging to some of the most affluent and powerful individuals in America, none of whom could be expected to welcome the appearance of an intrusive new building to spoil their view.

Stewart had initially commissioned the New York architect Walter Chatham to work on the restoration of the house. The exterior had to stay, and the rebuilt interior could not fight with it. The architecture of the interior had to have a sensibility that did not entirely reject the character of Bunshaft's challenging house, and yet it could not be an historical recreation of the original interior. Chatham did his best, but under the weight of all the baggage that came with the house, the project did not move on until the photographer, Todd Eberle (a frequent contributor to Stewart's magazine) suggested to Stewart that the architect who would know what to do with this difficult house was John Pawson.

It was, on the face of it, an unlikely commission. Stewart's taste, until this moment, had been identified with the decorative; her approach to architecture was apparently the mirror opposite of Pawson's rigour and asceticism. Nevertheless, Stewart was always interested in the idea of quality and, to her, Pawson was clearly the architect best able to deliver genuine spatial quality. As Pawson sees it, contemporary luxury in America is not about possessions, but about quality. 'People want the very, very best finishes and the very, very best spaces; that is luxury. That's what I'm offering – I'm offering space.'

Then Pawson had to consider the issue of over exposure and the way in which it could eat up the potency of his architecture. Pawson's work has moved steadily towards centre stage; to make a house for Martha Stewart would accelerate the process. Such a high-profile project could, in the long term, have the effect of leaving his architecture consumed by the very process of publicity, to become threadbare and stripped of meaning.

When Wakaba, the first restaurant that Pawson designed, opened in 1985, the reaction to it was characterized by authentic shock. 'It was based on an idea about what would make a nice restaurant that I had built up over a long period. Nobody had done it before in London, so it was easy to do something which really surprised people', says Pawson. 'Fifteen years later, there are just tons of spare minimal places. They are clean and pleasant, the Habitat version, you might say.'

For Pawson, the result has been to look for new ways of doing things that still keep his central objectives as their focus. 'It drives me to push myself further. People think it's just a matter of paint it white, put in a shadow gap, and not too much stuff. They think it is restrained, but being obsessed is the opposite of being restrained. The temptation is to use the same materials for every job, but you can't. No matter how much you say it's not a style, misuse does devalue things. It is very difficult, when you make one wrong choice of material you blow the whole thing.' But even now, after all the exposure in the magazines and the press, the white wall and shadow gap look is still confined to a certain taste culture. For a high-profile figure such as Martha Stewart to choose to identify herself with Pawson's work – to the extent of adopting his way of life in her own home – is to give it a much wider exposure, and possibly to transform its meaning.

The project began with a chance meeting between Stewart and Pawson in an East Hampton restaurant in the summer of 1995. It was followed by an invitation to a more formal conversation, when the Bunshaft House was discussed in detail. For an individual whose business is based so much on her own way of life, the remodelling of the Bunshaft House could not be anything but a major statement. With the huge readership of *Martha Stewart Living* peeking over the client's shoulder, it would never simply be a straightforward client-architect relationship. Pawson was aware that this would be a commission that might bring with it more than its fair share of complications. However, it was a project that, with its exceptional site and potential for a more than usually productive interchange with a client – clearly aware that the house would reflect on her professionally as well as personally – that seemed to be a risk

The house does not give up its secrets all at once. Only after you have negotiated the screen wall and reached the living room (shown here in its original state) facing the pond does the house finally reveal the view.

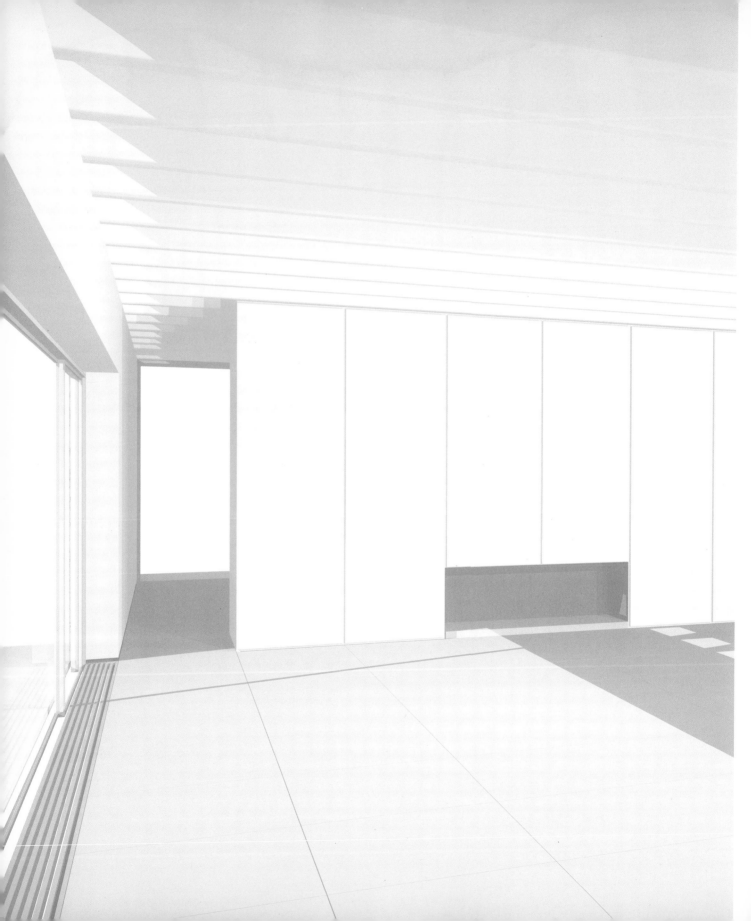

worth taking. Above all, he trusted Stewart. 'Martha is brilliant at merchandising. She has merchandised her home and her life, and everything into a magazine and a TV show. She is genuine, and she is thorough.' At a deeper level, there are parallels between Pawson's embrace of an architectural language, which is about a particular approach to domestic life, and Stewart's way of offering her readers the answers to the problems of how to live. Even if both of them approach the issue from different directions, they offer the promise of a solution to the messy complexity of everyday life. And both of them have their own, complete view of the world and the position of every object within it.

For Pawson, the idea that Stewart wanted to embrace the notion of simplicity came as no surprise. 'Everybody has the desire at some stage in their lives to have a clear out. The idea of simplification seems to appeal to people who have a trouble with choice.' According to Pawson, 'a lot of architecture is to do with making a series of choices.' His particular architecture is about making more choices than most. At the Georgica Pond project, however, it wasn't Pawson alone who was making the choices. 'Martha thought that she was going to learn something, that every decision for the house was going to be a process of shared discovery. For instance, for her studio overlooking the water I thought it would be nice to have wood on the floor … She wanted to be shown several woods, and make a choice. That is how she is used to working.' But it is by no means a phenomenon that is limited to Stewart. 'Every single client gets out a tape measure when you say the corridor will be three feet wide, you can see them visualizing it, they all want to be involved in the process.'

Before work started on the detailed design, there were a number of issues to resolve: the landmark

opposite The kitchen occupies a prominent position at the other end of the house, screened from the living area by a fireplace. Bathrooms and cloakrooms are grouped together into a single architectural element that serves to organize the space, defining a bedroom to one side, and the living room to the other.

status of the Bunshaft House; the sensitive ecology of the waterfront location; and the restrictions local zoning placed on development on the site. In sum, these meant that the original house had to stay, and that new development could only take the shape of a pool and a garage, and ancillary amenities associated with them. Pawson's strategy was to retain the existing structures, but to strip out their interiors to rebuild them, much in the same way as he has done in his own house in London.

The new building would be confined to the land side of the existing house, with pool huts and changing rooms organized around the pool. The new interventions and additions had to be sympathetic to Bunshaft's design and applied with a delicate touch. The original proportions, the sense of light and space, and the relationship of the house with its setting were sacrosanct. The new additions would update worn out technologies and materials. New accommodation was set away from the main house, with the extra space and facilities arranged so as to create a dignified new relationship between site, architecture and occupants.

The new work is conceived as a set of variations on Bunshaft's original theme; taking its lead from what is already there, but refining and exploring its language, while also bringing to it an architectural repertoire that is itself rooted in a sense of continuity and timelessness.

Pawson's reworking of the original programme groups bathrooms, laundry space and lavatories into a single square block that forms the only major architectural intrusion into the open interior of the house. It is positioned immediately facing the main entrance, and has the effect of creating a natural subdivision of spaces: the main sleeping space is to one side; the living area is at the centre of the house. The

opposite Due to the landmark status of the Bunshaft House, the new facilities – pool, cabanas and garage – had to be set away from the main house.
Each cabana is glazed on the pool-side elevation, and constructed from slabs of precast concrete to match the stone paving surrounding the pool.

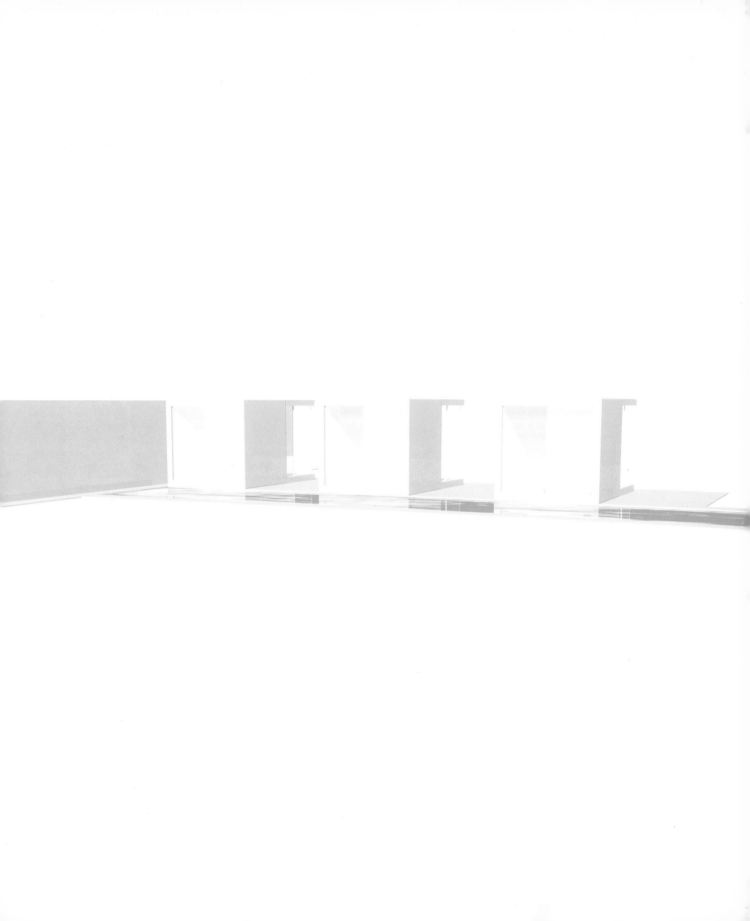

positioning of the cube has the effect of keeping alive Bunshaft's original idea – of only gradually revealing the water view. The kitchen is at the far end of the house, and has its own entrance. Work surfaces are parallel with the main frontage, and ensure that the cook gets the view as well as everybody else in the house. The kitchen is screened from the living area by a dividing wall that accommodates a fireplace at right angles to the long elevation.

The pool is set well back from the house but is linked to it by a careful network of paths and landscaping, and is itself screened from the road by trees and changing rooms. The rebuilt old studio is tied into his overall plan.

Pawson found the design process both intriguing and exhausting. 'When you design private houses, you cannot just follow a linear logical process. You cannot assume that, just because you have performed as well as you possibly can as an architect, the client will necessarily go along with what you suggest, because they don't. There is no set pattern when you are designing a private house. Your response comes from experience, from having built more than one house. You have to accept that the illogical is going to happen.' After considerable research, he suggested Indiana Limestone as the material for the interior of the main house. Stewart decided against it, however, as she had heard that Billy Joel had used the same stone for his patio, and it had cracked.

This house, which has had so much energy and care poured into it, has not yet been born. Building stopped the day, in the summer of 1998, that a dispute broke out between Stewart and a neighbour – one of those disputes that are apparently the inevitable product of the wealthy and powerful living in relatively close proximity. The neighbour was accustomed to having an empty house next door, and moved to protect his privacy when work started. He installed a wooden fence and planted a screen of trees. Stewart objected that the fence was partly on her land, and that it blocked her view of the water. The disagreement was eventually resolved in the courts. 'It, not unnaturally, somewhat depressed her', says Pawson, 'but it is entirely soluble. These are people who have proved that they can succeed incredibly well by not taking no for an answer. To suddenly back down over a fence, or to leave something less than perfect, as they see it, is not an option. If you are so successful, you are smart enough to listen to advice, but you have got to where you are by believing in yourself.' Such people have the determination and vision to make a one-off house working with the likes of Pawson. By the same token, it is their very determination which can make the course of building such a complex process.

One day, the house on Georgica Pond will be finished. Today, it is a quiet, peaceful island, a green lawn spilling forward from the house to the edge of the water. The shell of Bunshaft's house is intact: inside, it has been carefully scooped out, as another house waits to take shape within.

tilty barn

Essex is the most ambiguous of English counties. It is here that the urban, the suburban and the rural inhabit, not just the same village, but even the same lane. Elements of all three can rub shoulders within a single building. The rough sits cheek-by-jowl with the smooth. Steel windows and thatch, tractors and Range Rovers, claret and light ale coexist everywhere. It is a place characterized as much by ribbon development from the 1930s as by new towns from the 1960s. There are ancient Saxon churches and sprawling estates of executive homes. Its landscape is gentle and harsh all at the same time. It is a county in which you can find giant car factories and displaced Londoners working in them, as well as small holdings, farms and remote, isolated coastal communities. Art Deco stucco is never far away from ancient weathered brick.

What were once rural communities look, outwardly, much as they have for centuries; but in the last few decades they have been completely transformed by the arrival of new residents, many of whom make their living in the City, and by the collapse of the traditional agricultural economy. The old farm buildings once served to define the grain of the countryside; they created a grid laid across the landscape that formed the shape of daily life. But the farms that used them are disappearing, and the few surviving ones no longer have a use for the buildings.

The transformation of a disparate collection of agricultural buildings – on the edge of the straggling village of Tilty – into a home for a quintessentially metropolitan couple embodies many of these ambiguities. Working farms sit side by side with homes occupied by people whose work is so peripatetic that they can live anywhere they choose, and yet who still search for that elusive sense of rootedness that comes from village life.

Tilty Barn is the home of photographer Fi McGhee, graphic designer Sean Perkins and their young daughter Phoebe. Previously, they had lived in London, where they still have an office. McGhee works on location and in the studio at Tilty. Of equal importance to her work as a photographer is her passion for riding, and it was the decision to buy a horse that prompted the move to Essex. They found Tilty only after a protracted search through the area for the best combination of potential and value for money. More robustly handsome than picturesque, the string of farm buildings, separated from the original farmhouse, remained in working use until a decade ago. The oldest of them is an ancient timber-framed barn of considerable charm and historical interest. Its structure, concealed from the exterior under strips of sober black-painted lapped timber, explodes inside into an intricate three-dimensional spider's web of struts, ties and props that knits the roof into the wall. Warped and buckled with age, the original barn has been added to over the centuries in a number of distinct phases, each one supporting the next, and culminating in the newest, a stable block. It was built just a few decades ago and is now devoted to Klein, the black stallion that completes the household.

This was the raw material that Pawson was asked to turn into a home. When he saw it for the first time, it was still crusted with a thick coat of the accretions that had marked its changing use over the years. There was ancient farmyard mud and a less than watertight roof to deal with.

One of the first decisions to take was how much to keep of the existing structure. With all the mud and accumulated farmyard debris, it was hard to make out what there actually was to work with. The complex had grown by haphazard stages. Residential occupation

The barn, with its steeply pitched roof and timber frame, dates back to the eighteenth century and is the oldest of all of the farm buildings.

The barn, with its steeply
pitched roof, is to the right,
while the kitchen is in the
lower wing in the centre.
The stables are located
further down the incline.
Insertions into the original
fabric have a direct
robustness – new windows
are fitted directly into the
timber board cladding.

opposite The barn was
just one of a number of
agricultural buildings that
grew up over a long period.
The selective demolition of
later accretions revealed a
pleasingly regular plan with
a formal quality.

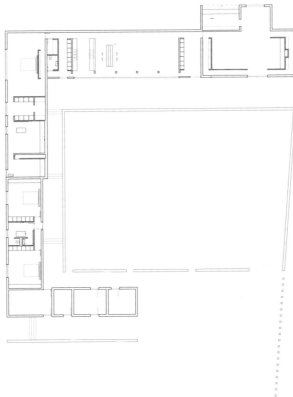

had never previously been an option, so there was a need to carry out a restructuring that made sense of all the disparate elements and put them to work in a new way, like a rural version of a New York loft.

Barns are ubiquitous in this part of Essex. Domesticating them has become a well-defined process, and it is regulated by a cautious planning regime. There is a protocol that accompanies the process. Large-scale new window openings are discouraged, as are supposedly unsympathetic materials. However, the results are not always as satisfactory as the authorities hope, even when the formula is followed to the letter. In too many cases, conversions have had the effect of extinguishing the innate qualities of the original barn, suburbanizing and prettifying what was once a simple and direct building type. Despite the absence of any overall conception, Tilty had the advantage of a plan that had acquired an underlying rectilinear clarity, even though it was the product of hundreds of years of haphazard accretions. Although there are other buildings close by, it had an outlook that focused not on the neighbouring settlement, but towards the open landscape.

The farm, positioned on top of a ridge, had formed a quadrangle of single-storey structures with one side left open. The oldest buildings, including the original barn, occupied the high ground, a low block stepped down the hill on one side, and the stables closed the courtyard at its lowest point. The complex was actually more like a rake of thin train carriages, strung out along a track, than a single building. There was a disarming directness about the way in which one space was attached to the next. The humility of the materials was equally appealing. These buildings were erected as a working environment, without artifice or

The inherent material qualities of vernacular agricultural buildings are sympathetically transformed by the creation of an all-glass wall to the kitchen and living area overlooking the courtyard.

above and previous page
Ancient beams in the barn,
with all their irregularities
and warped edges, form
a rich background to the
pristine geometry of
Pawson's new insertions.

pretension; and yet their generous proportions offered the potential, beneath the layers of makeshift alterations and decay, for the creation of architecture of genuine spatial quality. They were designed to accommodate livestock and produce rather than people, but their scale and size offered the potential for recasting them in a way that allowed their inherent character to speak for itself.

Having sketched out the basic structure of the house, carving out a quadrangle from the jumble of outhouses and creating a hard landscaped square from it, the most fundamental architectural decision was how to unlock this ribbon plan and bring to life the spaces it defined.

With all the spaces on one level, one opening onto the next, this was anything but a traditional house plan. The relationships of bedrooms to living room, kitchen to dining room, were established from scratch. At the same time, most of the buildings were so pinched in their width, that there was little room for manoeuvre in planning the circulation. The exposed timbers of the ancient barn, and its soaring interior, made it the dominant element. From whichever direction it was approached, it would be a magnetic draw pulling people inexorably towards it. The immediate questions were what to use it for, how to relate it to the main entrance and how it would address the rest of the spaces. By giving the barn too much predominance, for example by locating the main entrance into one of its walls, or by putting the kitchen in it, would mean that all the activities of the house would cluster there, leaving the rest of the complex underused and neglected. Yet to strip it of all clearly defined functions would marginalize it in the context of the overall complex.

The solution was to make the heart of the house an L-shaped range of accommodation. The old

barn is at one end, and the main entrance has been located in the middle of the link block, parallel with the barn, which connects it with the auxilliary accommodation that runs at right angles down the slope of the site. The house is approached from the courtyard side, away from the access road; most visitors do not come on foot, and the arrangement gives the house a sense of privacy. The door, a full-height opening cut in the wall, is camouflaged by lapped black timber boarding that matches the surrounding walls so exactly that it becomes invisible. Once inside, you find two vestigial walls that define a kind of entrance area which is still part of the main space that accommodates the kitchen. Bedrooms and bathrooms are allocated to the block running down the slope. The living room and an office are accommodated on the opposite side of this space, in the barn itself.

Each of these spaces has a different character and outlook. The bedrooms and bathrooms look straight out onto the open fields and floor-to-ceiling glass has the effect of making the landscape appear to be part of the interior and the field an extension of the floor. The kitchen looks down the slope towards the stable block and the hills beyond, yet the worktop, concealed in a single island, is positioned at right angles to the view. The barn is a more introverted space in which the qualities of the exposed rafters predominate, but because of its position, it acts as the climax to a journey through the house. Visually, it is held in reserve, biding its time, rather than making itself immediately obvious. Throughout, cupboards and storage are kept out of the major spaces and concentrated behind walls or in subsidiary spaces.

To tie all this together, the floor is simple poured concrete throughout. With such an extensive floor area, the budget didn't run to anything richer, but it

A rough timber structure in the roof provides a counterpoint to the smooth poured concrete floor. The glass wall integrates the courtyard with one of the main living areas of the house, while the sheltering brick wings outside provide a sense of security and visual privacy.

previous page View from the main bedroom. All of the bedrooms look out over open fields. A range of rooms open one into another moving down the slope.

is a material that reflects the plain, direct quality of the barn. The roof itself has been left intact, so that it comes down low over the window wall. Everywhere, the insertions are kept to a minimum. The new domestic use for the old agricultural structures does not seek to impose a new aesthetic on them; rather it explores their inherent qualities. From the way you are led from one space to the next, you become aware of their individual character and of the transition between them. A storage room and a lavatory form a barrier to insulate the kitchen space from the bedrooms. The two bedrooms are insulated, one from the other, by a bathroom in which the lavatory is accommodated in a stone bench that matches the stone bath box. The palette of materials is kept deliberately low key. The most precious insertions, such as the Carrara marble wash basin, are concealed from the main space, and made to seem more precious by being housed inside a plain walled box of a room, almost as if it were a casket. The only overtly architectural intervention on the exterior is the glass that is applied externally over the window openings which look out over the fields. There is no frame and no edge detail, as though the glass were protecting a canvas of a landscape. The insertions in the barn take the opposite tack; new low walls are used to create a quiet void in the centre of the space, oriented around a new fireplace. They have the paradoxical effect of cocooning the richness of the wall timbers in a series of intense subsidiary spaces around the edges of the room, characterized by the tensions between rough timbers and smooth late twentieth-century plaster.

This is a house that is about the qualities of materials and creates a sense of space and calmness; it is integrated with its setting, and it makes the most of unconventional interiors.

View from the main bedroom looking towards the bathroom. The washbasin at the end of the corridor is carved from a single block of York stone.

jigsaw

Bond Street, once one of London's most traditional shopping streets, has metamorphosed over the last decade to join the handful of addresses that receive instant recognition throughout the fashion world. It is a modestly scaled street that still reflects the proportions of the brick and stucco eighteenth-century townhouses that used to line it. Architecturally, it is more mixed now, with Victorian ceramic-tiled facades alternating with frowzy early twentieth-century classicism, and the occasional lump from the 1960s. In typical English style, it meanders in leisurely fashion from Oxford Street, at one end, to Piccadilly at the other.

Bond Street is now in the same league as the via Montenapoleone in Milan and Rodeo Drive in Beverly Hills. It is the street name that retailers go out of their way to get a chance to print on their heavy, gloss-coated, rope-handled shopping bags. They use it to signal, unambiguously, that they are in the big time. The banks, furniture showrooms and travel agents that used to dominate the area have been driven out by Ralph Lauren, Gianni Versace and Donna Karan, in a contemporary version of the clustering together of trades in single streets that shaped medieval cities.

The big names congregate together, but they also compete with each other in an effort to create ever bigger and more impressive stores. For a fashion retailer, to open on Bond Street is to make a statement; each new opening attempts to upstage the last. They are, after all, targeting an audience that is more than usually sensitized to the nuances and meanings of style, and represent an industry that is constantly looking for new ways of impressing and entertaining its jaded customers. The more fashion names attracted to the area, the more the rents rise, and the more painful becomes the price of entry for newcomers.

It is not just the international celebrity designers that set up in Bond Street, or its vicinity. Those mainstream domestic retailers that aspire to the same fashionable gloss as the international names like to be close by too. Certainly the Jigsaw chain was making a statement about itself when it opened up in Bond Street in 1996. It is a British-owned company that started out in the 1970s by targeting the affluent suburbs, beginning with Hampstead and Putney. Jigsaw offers a distinctive brand of chic but affordable clothes. It has built its success on shops that look stylish, but do not intimidate the customers and sells own brand clothes that are fashionable but not extreme. Critically, it has appealed to its audience by concentrating on creating an attractive image for its label, rather than investing in the individual signature of a big name designer and all the elaborate paraphernalia of catwalks and collections that go with it.

As such, it is inevitably a follower and an interpreter of the twists and turns of fashion rather than a leader or an agenda setter. Coming to Bond Street was a business decision. The store had to recoup its investment in property, which was much greater than a typical Jigsaw outlet, while still selling its products at exactly the same price as they are in Bristol or Manchester. However, it would also be able to use the new store to do something to affect perceptions among potential customers of its other, perhaps more typical outlets. They would all be able to share in some of the reflected gloss of the Bond Street address; and in the crowded high street, Jigsaw was moving just a little up market, ahead of its competitors. Without wanting to intimidate, the look of the store was beginning to ask customers to look at its clothes in a slightly different way.

Jigsaw had thirty-eight outlets by the time it reached Bond Street. It had already established itself in

towns from Brighton to Glasgow, in high streets and
shopping malls. Even in this context, it always tried to
set itself apart from the conventional norms of mass
market retailing. It developed its own distinctive personality that was based neither on the cosmetic paint job of
a one-off independent, nor on the off-the-shelf retailing
solutions of the multiples designed not to offend anyone.

As the company matured, it began to consider its
architectural image with increasing attention. Jigsaw
has avoided a single style for its stores. British designer
Nigel Coates, of Branson Coates, was commissioned to
design their Knightsbridge and Kensington stores, and
attracted considerable attention with them. They stood
out for their painterly use of materials and distinctly
exotic identities; Coates came up with a look that was
two parts Gaudí to one part Casbah. Then Pawson was
commissioned for Bond Street. Certainly there is not
much common ground between Branson Coates' flam-
boyant patinated copper, decorative wrought iron and
custard-yellow painted walls and Pawson's much more
austere architecture. But whatever their differences,
neither architect is part of the conventional retailing
world, and both bring their own distinctive approach to
interiors. 'We want the shops to look different to express
their individuality,' says Jigsaw's owner John Robinson.

The site in Bond Street had previously been
a photographic retail store. It had been the subject of a
series of makeshift and unsympathetic conversions over
the years. Two domestically scaled nineteenth-century
buildings, one stone-faced, the other with a brick
facade, had been unceremoniously shoved together to
form a single property. A procession of owners had all
left their own contradictory marks on it. The building
employed the typical high street trick of encouraging
window shoppers with a shop front that went from the

Jigsaw's London flagship
was a conversion of a
conversion. Two disparate
adjoining structures in
Bond Street had already
been knocked into one.
There had been an attempt
to deal with the architectural incongruity of the
situation at street level by
grafting a new frontage
across both buildings.
Pawson's design, inside
and out, took the process
several steps further,
uniting basement and
ground floor by cutting
back the existing structure.

pavement to plunge deep into the interior of the store, past a procession of crowded display cases. There was a brash plastic fascia plastered across both frontages, in a largely futile attempt to make them read as one. Once past the frontage, the shop straggled a long way back from the street in a plan that tapered to a narrow rear section. It was encrusted with incoherent additions and confused alterations. In material terms, it felt deeply uncomfortable under a layer of plastic and asbestos tile, and lit by harsh fluorescent strips.

Pawson's strategy was to cut away the clutter, and go back to the underlying qualities of the interior. It was a project that meant working with the grain of the building, rather than against it. The point was to respect the scale and proportions of the facade and rescue it from the mess, rather than to impose an alien aesthetic on it. 'I worked by taking things out, not by putting them in', says Pawson. The existing frontage has been stripped away and a new facade created that addresses the original architecture of the two buildings, and provides an appropriate new entrance, one that strikes a balance between solid wall and transparent window. The openings in the front wall have been concentrated in twin apertures that are framed with simple Portland stone panels rising two floors up. Office space and a press room went on the upper floors, and the first floor was cut back to create a double-height, 6-metre tall entrance, making room for displays and installations. The windows are further defined by bronze mullions and a bronze plinth, partly to respect the insistence of the planning authority on a facade treatment which did not create too wide a dissonance between street facades and upper levels. The entrance is on the left hand side, through a pair of full-height glass doors. The intention to create retail space on two levels, the women's collection

opposite The unsympathetic alterations to the ground floor of two domestically scaled buildings have been unified into two matching stone-edged, bronze-trimmed windows on Bond Street.

below Looking back toward the front of the store, and its window to Bond Street, the etched acrylic screens create a series of discrete spaces, in which the walnut shelves display the Jigsaw range in edited groups.

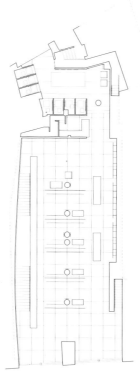

opposite A double staircase leading from the back and the front of the shop connects Jigsaw's two floors. Jigsaw is careful to distance itself from the high street chains; it uses architecture to differentiate itself, and to ensure that no two stores are exactly the same.

right The upper level is defined by its unifying granite floor, with full-height translucent screens used to create discrete areas for displaying various selections of the range.

on the ground floor, with men's clothes in the basement, was later changed. Men's clothes are now in a separate store of their own around the corner. But there is still a clear distinction between the two levels, both in materials and spatial quality.

Once the clutter had been stripped out, the plan was revealed as fundamentally irregular. Neither of the two party walls were parallel, and they cranked back and forth as the interior opened out; nor were they at right angles to the facade. Rather than bury these walls under an orthogonal geometry, the new plan accommodates these irregularities. On the ground floor, Pawson used a stone floor as a unifying element, and stopped it short of the smooth white finished walls. By placing diffused lighting in the slot between walls and floor, the irregularity is controlled and contained, and the wall seems to float free of the floor. Bush hammered granite was used, stretching more than 30 metres all the way from the street to the back of the store. The stone is kept free of unnecessary intrusions, and treated in such a way as to make the material feel like a solid, massive and continuous surface rather than thin tiles. It gives a sense of permanence that is especially important for a fashion shop, which can be overwhelmed by a rapid turnover of visual imagery.

Under layers of succeeding alterations and redecoration, the interiors had lost all sense of character and definition. Pawson's design attempted to create a series of interrelated spaces of real quality. It was not possible to remove all the columns, nor could all the walls simply be scooped out. Instead, they are incorporated into the new interior as unobtrusively as possible. The idea was to make the space simple, to hide all the inessential visual clutter of air-conditioning ducts and sprinklers that infest even, what are otherwise, the most carefully considered of interiors. There is a tendency to assume, just because grilles, ducts and lighting systems are so universal, that they are invisible; this is anything but true. Getting rid of them, to achieve a smooth white ceiling that floats uninterrupted, free of walls and partitions, is a remarkably effective way of liberating space.

In the lower level, the floor is laid with douglas fir planks as wide and as long as possible to stretch from front to back. Timber used in this way gives a sense of the essence of the material, of its thickness and the scale of the trees from which it has been cut. There is a deliberate contrast between stone and timber between the two floors; the materials play against each other.

Ground floor and basement levels are connected by a monumental pair of staircases positioned against one wall. One starts from the front of the shop, the other from the back, both descending to meet at a landing from which a short third flight takes off at a right angle to deliver customers to the centre stage of the lower floor. 'I like staircases that give you a sense of transition', says Pawson. 'I like that feeling of passing through the thickness of a wall. Moving between the entrance level and the lower floor, you feel the pressure of the massive walls that flank the stairs.'

It was also important to make the shop easy for its customers to understand and to use. The ground floor is planned around four distinct display areas set between, on one side, a long low shelving unit that stretches back into the shop, along the line of the staircase, and on the other, two long tables. Each area is defined by a full-height, hand-etched acrylic screen that provides a sense of enclosure, minimizes the visual impact of necessary structural columns and provides a background to the display forms. Each of the screens is lit from floor level, making them appear to float,

Etched glass screens sub-
divide the space on the
ground floor, but in the
Bond Street Jigsaw, it is
the staircase linking the
two that is the principle
architectural experience.

suffused with a gentle glow. Within each area, displays are used to convey the theme of a particular range of styles, which shoppers are able to select for themselves by picking individual items from the length of shelving nearest the display and from the hanging rails. They assemble their selection on the tables that act almost as shopping baskets, before taking the clothes to the changing area at the back of the store to try them on.

General illumination is achieved by continuous wall washing, with no scalloping, from fittings positioned in a slot running the length of the walls. Additional secondary lighting to highlight clothes is hung within the niche on the right-hand wall. The cash and wrap area, with comfortable seating, is positioned towards the rear of the store, screening the changing area at the very back which has natural light. For the lower sales floor, changing rooms are at the front with cash and wrap at the back. An array of tables, hanging rails, and display and storage shelves provides the same pattern for retailing and atmosphere as that established on the upper level.

Jigsaw chose Pawson to create a shop that would reflect a step further into the fashion big league; a choice that was far from accidental. While Jigsaw may not necessarily put it in so many words, if the Bond Street shop ended up looking as much a piece of architecture by Pawson as a Jigsaw shop, it wasn't going to be a problem. It was Pawson's signature that Jigsaw was looking for; it had got the right site, and it wanted the right architect to give it the right, fashion-conscious look. A successful result would give a lift to every item it sold and to the whole chain. That look has subsequently become an essential part of the company's image, and, when Jigsaw expanded with a series of stores in Japan, the company went back to Pawson to design them.

The first floor, on which the Jigsaw press room is located, has been cut back at the entrance window wall, to allow the first impression of the store to be characterized by a generously proportioned double-height space.

pawson house

In the basement of his office just behind King's Cross station, John Pawson has rows and rows of neatly ordered shelves filled with uniformly bound volumes documenting every design that he has ever worked on. None of the carefully indexed files, with their white spines and sans serif typography, occupy more space than the set that records three years' work on his own house in west London. The earliest file begins with a set of the estate agent's particulars, annotated in Pawson's distinctive handwriting. A glossy colour snapshot is attached to two sheets of brief details describing tiled kitchens and guest cloakrooms. It shows a flat-fronted, stucco terraced house, no different from thousands of others built right across the suburbs of west London throughout most of the nineteenth century; a house that, in essence, has ceased to exist. It used to belong to a journalist, and was decorated in a style that suggested a down-at-heel wine bar of the 1970s. There follows a series of photocopies of ancient maps that show, in freeze-frame manner, the rapid development of Notting Hill. Shortly before the house was built, it was an area of smoke-belching brick yards and pottery workshops set in open fields; by 1830, they were rapidly being swallowed up by an exploding city expanding inexorably westward.

By the time Queen Victoria came to the throne, there was an attempt to put some of the land to more salubrious use. A racecourse was laid out, which did a lot to make the atmosphere less polluted. Perhaps as a result, the land was quickly bought up by speculative house builders. They laid out a grid of streets across the whole area, obliterating the turf with new roads and creating raised pavements from the soil they excavated for strip foundations for new houses.

The house forms part of a long rectangle of terraces facing outwards on four sides of a private com-

The house was the product of a nineteenth-century pattern book design. Cracked lintels betrayed structural problems that Pawson had to address.

munal garden, inverting the usual pattern of the London square. Pawson's street is one of the short sides, but only a single pair of what was clearly meant to a be larger terrace of houses was actually built before the receiver was called in. The houses remained unsold for nearly ten years afterwards.

The report continues with a discursive analysis of the history of London's domestic architecture. Over the years, reckless commercial expediency was tempered by an evolving set of by-laws, mainly based on issues of health and fire safety; these led to the gradual adoption of a standard house pattern capable of being repeated at a variety of scales in huge numbers, depending on the affluence of the market the builder was targeting. There are perhaps five basic versions of the terraced house in London of increasing scale and size. Pawson's, when it was built, was not quite the cheapest, but it was still modest. It was a cottage, really, but scaled up a little to adopt an urban quality, and dignified with a vestigial classical reference or two around the entrance and front windows. Inside, it had just two rooms on each of the four floors, a basement dug into the ground, a staircase winding up the party wall and a valley-pitched, slate-covered roof. In all, it had no more than 150m^2 of space, in which a family of as many as eight people might have lived together, with two or perhaps even three servants.

Next in the file is a set of satellite photographs showing the house and its surroundings from ten miles up. There is also a copy of a geological survey, initially prompted by the need to deal with the all too visible case of subsidence that had deterred every other prospective purchaser. Pawson didn't stop with just a look at the state of the clay underneath the rudimentary strip footings that the Victorians had skimped on to such predictable effect. He wanted a bore hole dug to determine how far down he would have to go to be able to extract geothermal heat to warm the house.

Then there are the dozens of bound volumes that show all the drawings that have been used to chart the progress of the design. As well as plans, elevations and sections, each room, and each space that connects them, is also rendered in three-dimensional line drawings that explore the relationships of one room to another, and each element in that room to every other element. There are files full of beautifully photographed images of the models that were made to explore the design. Even more pictures show the progress of construction. These are not the usual site photographs taken mechanically as a contractual record – they have an aesthetic quality of their own. You get the feeling that it is not enough for a space to look right only when it is finally finished, it has to look right on the way to getting there. In addition to the files, there are rows of video tapes that portray the site work and more images of the finished space.

All the files, and records and exploration might be seen as the act of an obsessive, but it doesn't feel in the least excessive, or superfluous. However, it clearly isn't simply a pragmatic working method either; it is also done for its own sake. Pawson is trying to explore the essence of every aspect of the project, to extract every possible scrap of architectural meaning in order to help shape his decisions about the design. It allows him to brief his assistants to explore in detail the implications of his decisions and to evaluate their ideas.

An architect's house all too often serves as a self-advertisement, which is not an outcome with which Pawson would feel comfortable. A house is a place in which to live, more than an investment, financial or professional. He has designed more than enough homes

Though on the modest scale of a cottage, Pawson's house belongs to a tradition of London domestic architecture that used classical embellishments – from pillars at the door, to cornices around the windows – in the pursuit of urban dignity. On the exterior there is little evidence of the remodelling of the interior.

for his own and his family's use – as well as for a wide range of the most demanding of clients – to have extinguished any temptation towards exhibitionism. 'Designing for yourself is like a doctor operating on his family. You set yourself ridiculously ambitious targets. You can't just do it the right way, you have to find the very best solution, so you go through all the possibilities.'

For Pawson, architecture is a direct reflection of an attitude towards life. It is an expression of a search for order, of taking pleasure in the complexity of simplicity, of restraint and the suppression of excess and ostentation. His own home is as eloquent a summation of those architectural values as he can make it. 'My premise has always been that your work must reflect your character, but completing the house has been a bit of a shock. I didn't realize that you have to learn to live in your own things, and I will make some changes.'

Of course a house must be, at least in part, autobiographical. It is a reflection of both who we are and who we want to be. In that sense, Pawson is a distinctive personality. Long before he actually became an architect, he had started to tinker with domestic interiors. The family home was old, made of stone and, though its grounds were being gradually encroached on by the growth of Halifax, it retained a certain dignity. As his siblings began to leave home, Pawson got a bigger room, then knocked some walls down. 'I had a room the size of a drawing room eventually, and decided not to fill it up. It was just a single bed in a giant room.' Then he moved into a cottage in the grounds. 'Dad had designed and built it. I set about changing it, which gave him a bit of a shock, especially when I took out the inglenook, and put in a simple cantilevered slate bench.'

By the time that Pawson got started on the house, he had designed places to live for individuals as

A subsidence problem meant that the house would need underpinning, but a design that included stone floors throughout would require a completely new structural frame. With the interior hollowed out, and the old staircase removed, the house is ready for a new interior that nevertheless leaves the old skin intact.

demanding and individualistic as the writer Bruce Chatwin and the collector Doris Saatchi. On three different occasions, he had designed homes in which he lived himself; in Elvaston Place, Drayton Gardens and Redcliffe Square – one in a house converted into flats and two in a block of mansion flats.

This is the second London terraced house that Pawson and his interior designer wife, Catherine, have lived in. The first was in Stoneleigh Street, a simple brick terrace built at the end of the nineteenth century. This house, close by but in a quieter area, is not much larger. Perhaps fifty years older, it was built with considerably more social and architectural ambition, despite its modest proportions. Neither house was apparently much concerned with the inspirations that shape Pawson's architecture. Yet they were both reordered as powerful, intensely-felt architectural expressions. There is something in the very modesty of the setting that powerfully demonstrates the fact that the clarity Pawson seeks in every detail has a wider relevance. The fact that modest spaces and everyday materials can be so completely transformed, is a demonstration of this and of Pawson's architectural integrity. His approach to design is painstaking, a question of assessing every possible outcome of a decision and of considering every potential solution before moving forward.

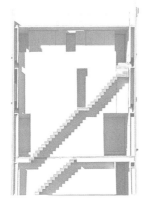

The street's orientation, as Catherine Pawson immediately spotted, transformed the standardized plan into something out of the ordinary. Although it appears to sit on a conventional London street, it backs onto a hidden communal garden at the rear, and its front looks over more communal gardens without any intervening houses. As a result, the sky and green lawns form most of its outlook, front and back. It feels like a free-standing house in a landscape, not part of a terrace. Yet the plan was utterly conventional; a whole family and its servants would have been wedged into the confining restraint of two blank walls, barely 5 metres apart, just wide enough to accommodate a room, corridor and staircase. The main level opened onto the street at the front and had the best proportioned and lightest rooms. Yet access to the gardens and the communal gardens beyond is from the basement which, at the front, is confronted by a blank subterranean retaining wall. For almost two centuries this basic form, replicated at a variety of scales, was the universal London house.

      Every conceivable strategy to transform this old generic house plan to accommodate individual requirements has been explored. Is the basement level, with direct access to the garden, the most appropriate place to put the kitchen and main living space, even though it is usually darker and not as well proportioned as the space above? Or perhaps these rooms should go on the ground floor level which, though it is certainly lighter and has higher ceilings, does not allow you to step out directly into the garden. And, since the kitchen has been turned into the *de facto* heart of the middle-class home, should it be moved up onto the principal floor to take over the space that was once occupied by the old living and drawing rooms? If so, then what happens to the basement; will people really go down a staircase from the kitchen to eat their meals or relax in front of a TV? Or would it be abandoned and simply used as an access route to the garden? Is the most appropriate strategy a reconstruction that ignores existing grain and fabric, or should the architect attempt to work with what he finds and make the most of its innate qualities?

      The new house was bought in a hurry after the Stoneleigh Street property sold unexpectedly quickly, and the Pawsons moved in almost at once, after a fast

The key design decision was to include a new staircase, allowing for a much freer treatment of the plan on each level. A straight flight, accessed from the rear, rises the whole way up the house. Underneath, another flight goes down to the kitchen, on the garden level.

paint and carpet job made it temporarily habitable. The pause before work started gave them a chance to think about what they needed from the new place. 'You find yourself asking, why have we moved, and why is it that we move every five years? This is what the brief is actually about. What do you really need, what do you really want. Very few people sit down and analyse it that way.'

A period of reflection gave Pawson the time to consider strategies. The existing stairs were attractive enough to consider retaining, but to do so would have frozen the plan. Keeping them would mean that the plan would always suffer from a less than ideal L-shape. Replacing the old stairs with a single straight flight climbing all the way up the house from the ground floor, and a second flight underneath it to reach the basement level, opened up the plan – it offered a 4-metre wide band of unencumbered space. To make sure that it was entirely unencumbered, Pawson went to the extent of cutting notches in the walls in which to bury service pipes and flues. Not even a duct or a pipe would be allowed to intrude into the spatial purity of the interior. From that decision everything else followed, reinforcing the fact that the greatest asset of the house was its location. The facades were protected by planning legislation, but everything else could be removed to meet the brief that the Pawsons devised. 'People don't use the word site much about a terraced house in London, but that is what it is in this case. In Los Angeles, they talk about a tear down when it is the land that counts, not what is on it. In that sense, this is a tear down.'

Ultimately, the point of the exercise was to address the needs of the family; two adults and the children. The key advantage to be gained in moving from the last house was to make a home that would be a good

The traditional terraced London house offers the tightest of constraints: two rooms on each floor, bounded by tight party walls and defined by a staircase. With a series of deft transformations, Pawson has given the familiar formula an entirely different character.

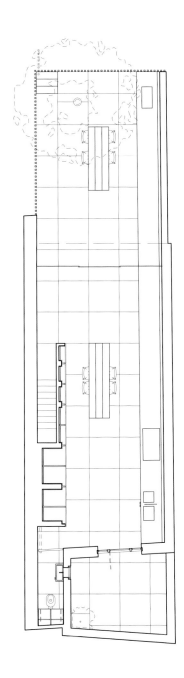

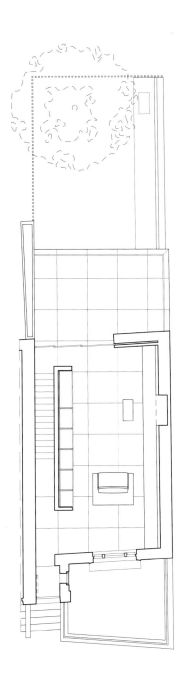

left The living room
occupies the whole of the
ground floor and opens out
onto the terrace beyond.
The stone bench in front
of the hearth runs the
length of the room, and
is a prominent part of
the design.

opposite Stone stairs rise
between two sheer white
walls. The last few treads
wind around to reach the
top floor. On the way up,
there is an opening in the
wall at landing level, which
leads into the parents'
bedroom.

place in which to bring up children. And it was this that made the communal garden so appealing. It offers them a safe place to play and to make friends of their own age from the other houses surrounding the gardens. Pawson calls it the English version of communal living Le Corbusier style. It offers the benefit of having both a small private garden at the same time as a communal green space almost big enough to get lost in.

'The houses in the area are all similar, and almost all have been added to and altered over the years. Everybody does their own version of remodelling and updating the basic plan. Most extend the basement level into the back garden, which at the same time provides a terrace on top. Some put conservatories or glass houses at the back of the main house. The overriding idea seems to be that family life happens in the basement', says Pawson. 'It's sad in a way, to look out of our windows and rarely see people using all that space on the raised ground floor. Sometimes you may see the man reading a book, late, after dinner, while his partner is downstairs, but mostly they just don't get used. In a way it would be better if the living room and the kitchen were combined.'

The changes in technology introduced into the home since the original house was built offer the architect considerable freedom, despite the restricted dimensions of the plan. Modern plumbing allows for a shower or a WC to be installed just about anywhere, fireplaces are no longer strictly necessary and built-in cupboards take the place of wardrobes and can also accommodate the appliances that have supplanted the traditional laundry. There is no staff to accommodate, no need for a maid's room, so they don't need quarters; or a place for them to be during the day, so it is possible to combine kitchen and dining areas.

The main bedroom has a bed at the back and the bath at the front, separated by a dividing bank of full-height wardrobes. The original front and back walls were not at right angles to the party wall, and Pawson's stone bath tapers to accommodate this geometry.

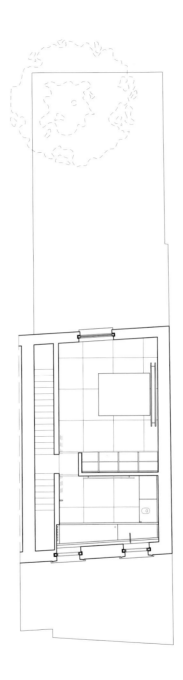

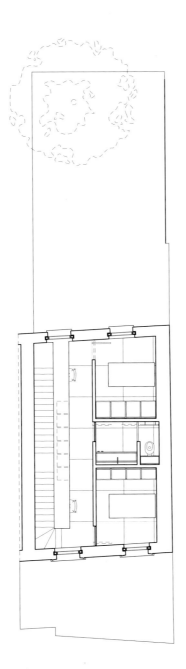

opposite and overleaf At the back of the house, the ground-floor kitchen has been projected forward into the garden, creating a terrace above it. The division between interior and exterior is minimized to the point that the distinction all but disappears. Pawson's Obumex kitchen runs the length of one wall and appears to run into the garden.

left The two children's bedrooms, divided by a shower, are on the top floor. A bench runs the whole length of the stairwell and provides a work area.

The removal of the stairs freed up the whole house, but it left the question of how to arrange activities on each level. The first issue was to resolve the relationship between the children's and the parents' bedrooms. Then there is the relationship between kitchen and living rooms. 'You are living with three other people, so you have to think about how you cope with teenagers creeping past your bedroom door on the way up to their bedroom. If you orientate the stairs in such a way that it means going through the living room, there is always going to be a need for compromise. You can't just design a house for entertaining. It has got to be enjoyable for 24 hours a day, and 365 days in the year. We thought we could be on the top floor and do something with the roof. But Catherine would sooner the boys pass us than we pass them on the way to bed.' Thus adults are on the second floor, children at the top. Then there was the relationship between the kitchen and the living area. 'I tried to see if I could combine the basement and the first floor, but there is not enough space to do that comfortably.'

With those basic decisions made, the rest fell into place. 'It enabled us to say, this room is going to be used for sitting and drinking. This terrace is bound, at some point, to have a table. The basement is the easy one to rationalize. You have the stairs, and everything else is parallel to the walls. The kitchen is against the wall, there is a dining area and provision for outside dining. It becomes quite clear what will happen down here, it will be homework, and most of the meals and the entertaining. If you put in a single flight of stairs, it means you can accommodate bedrooms on the top floor at the front and the back with a shower room in between, with a roof light above, and a worktop running the length of the stairs. You can open the whole of the roof over the shower on the top floor, so in summer you can shower in the open. I don't have a problem going up there.'

Then there is the detail of the private rooms to consider. Should the main bedroom and bathroom be a single space, running from the back to the front of the house, offering the attractions of a dual aspect; or should it be subdivided? 'You have an open space 4 metres by 8 metres. It is a double square, but how do you incorporate bed, bath and storage in that space. There is a great thing about being able to look both ways, to have a dual aspect, but at the same time you have to have adequate storage, so where do you put it if you aren't going to spoil the proportions? Something has got to give.' Pawson's drawings explored both possibilities. In the end, the bedroom is at the back of the house, with the view of sky and trees filling the window when seen from the bed, and the bathroom is at the front, with a tapering stone trough that feels almost Roman in its simple, massive quality. And there is storage space between the two.

Then there is the question of materials. If the interior floors are wood then, given Pawson's belief in making things as simple as possible with as few junctions and interruptions as he can manage, the garden should be floored in wood too, and the area at the front as well. In the end, Pawson chose stone. 'Wood outside a Victorian house doesn't seem right, so it makes it logical to make the kitchen and dining room stone.' There is a stone floor throughout, supported by a concrete frame and 3 metres of underpinning, necessary as the stone floors and stairs weigh as much as the rest of the house.

The house plan is narrow and almost twice as deep as its restricted frontage is wide. Pawson worked to dispel the tunnel-like quality that might have resulted by creating a series of vistas and views, both internally

previous page and overleaf The main entrance to the house is marked by the view of the underside of the stairs climbing in a straight flight. It opens onto the living room, for which Pawson has designed a new fireplace and a sofa which can also function as a desk. The sofa-desk was developed for Driade, the Italian furniture manufacturer.

and externally. 'What I'm trying to achieve is a series of private and calm spaces. I want an empty room, with just a bed in it. I want to be able to walk into a room that is only a shell. I don't want to have a cubicle in it. It is a balance; you want that feeling of space and calmness. But living in a loft in one big room with everything in it is not necessarily the answer. The advantage of having all the levels in the house is that, in a sense, you don't need a wall, because the floor does the job for you.'

Like many of Pawson's designs, on entering the house you find yourself in what feels like an airlock, or decontamination chamber. When you have adjusted to this first transition, you are confronted by the underside of two flights of stone steps, thick blocks that span across a slot rising the whole 12-metre height of the house. It allows light to filter down, as the steps appear to cascade overhead. Pawson calls it an entrance hall, which is what it is, on an heroic scale despite its restricted dimensions.

Sitting in the living room, on the oak sofa that Pawson designed for himself, looking out across the warm, luminous cream stone floor to the view of intense green in the garden and the sky above it, or walking down the cascade of stone steps into the level below where the kitchen worktop extrudes effortlessly through the glass wall at the rear and on towards visual infinity outside, it is hard to believe that this house was once a shoe box. Instead it is a place of extraordinary spatial freedom, of permanence and peace. However, the contrast between present and past doesn't feel like a conjuring trick, or a sleight of hand. The feeling is more, perhaps, that the architect has revealed what was already there.

selected works

1981
van Royen Apartment
Hester van Royen
London

1982
Chatwin Apartment
Bruce Chatwin
London

1983
Waddington Galleries
Leslie Waddington
London

1984
Audi Apartment
Pierre Audi
London

Boilerhouse Exhibition
Victoria & Albert Museum
London

1985
Waddington Apartment
Ferriel Waddington
London

van Royen Apartment
Hester van Royen
London

1986
Abu Saad Apartment
Lelia and Walid Abu Saad
London

Waddington House
Clodagh and Leslie
Waddington
London

JCB Visitor Centre Project
JCB
Rochester
(unbuilt)

Objects Exhibitions
Environment
London

PPOW Gallery
Penny Wilkington and
Wendy Olsdorf
New York

1987
Neuendorf Apartment
Carolina and Hans
Neuendorf
Frankfurt

Saatchi House
Doris Saatchi
London

Bock Apartment
Vivienne Bock
London

Wakaba Restaurant
Kieko and Minoru
Yoshihara
London

1988
Miro House
Victoria and Warren Miro
London

Craig-Martin Studio
Michael Craig-Martin
London

Starkmann Offices
Starkmann Library Services
London

Cannelle Cakeshop
Raja Cortas
London

Runkel Hue-Williams
Gallery
Claus Runkel and Michael
Hue-Williams
London

1989
Neuendorf House
Carolina and Hans
Neuendorf
Majorca

Neuendorf Art Centre
Hans Neuendorf
Germany
(unbuilt)

1990
Rothman Apartment
Florence and Noel
Rothman
London

Fusion Gallery
Dominic Berning
London

Connaught Brown Gallery
Anthony Brown
London

1991
van Royen Apartment
Hester van Royen
London

RK RK Shop
Rajindra Dhawan
London

1992
Wagamama Restaurant
Alan Yau
London

1993
Audi House
Pierre Audi
Amsterdam

Donnelly House
Marie and Joe Donnelly
Dublin

Tarn House
Gary Tarn
London

1994
Pawson House
Catherine and John
Pawson
London

Calvin Klein Store
Calvin Klein Inc
Tokyo

The Raw and the Cooked
Exhibition
Museum of Modern Art
Oxford

1995
Tilty Barn
Fi McGhee and Sean
Perkins
Essex

Jurgen Lehl Store
Jurgen Lehl Co
Kumamoto

GAM Conference Suite
Gilbert de Botton
London

Calvin Klein Store
Calvin Klein Inc
New York

Sun Assurance Building
Bernhard van Moerkerke
Ostend
(unbuilt)

1996
van Moerkerke House
Sophie van Moerkerke
London

Zander House
David Zander
Los Angeles
(unbuilt)

Donnelly House
Marie and Joe Donnelly
Dublin
(unbuilt)

Palmano House
Cindy Palmano
London

Calvin Klein Store
Calvin Klein Inc
Seoul

Jigsaw Store
Robinson Webster
Holdings
London

Jigsaw Store
Marui Trading Japan
Yokohama

Jigsaw Store
Marui Trading Japan
Shizuoka

Obumex Kitchen System
Obumex
Belgium

Michael Hue-Williams
Gallery
Michael Hue-Williams
London

GOMA Exhibition
Glasgow 1999
Glasgow

Martin Smith Exhibition
Boijmans Museum
Rotterdam

New Times New Thinking
Exhibition
Crafts Council
London

1997
Lucy Rie and Hans Coper
Exhibition
Barbican Arts Centre
London

1998
Mas des Predelles
Janet and Gilbert de Botton
Provence

7L bookshop, studio and
apartment
Karl Lagerfeld
Paris
(unbuilt)

El Horria guesthouses,
pool and studio
Karl Lagerfeld
Biarritz
(unbuilt)

Cathay Pacific Lounges
Cathay Pacific
Hong Kong

Calvin Klein Men's Store
Calvin Klein Inc
Paris

1999
Beekman Place Apartment
Melissa Evins
New York

Faggionato Apartment
Anne Faggionato and
Mungo Park
London

Pawson House
Catherine and John Pawson
London

Glynn House
Lisa and Richard Glynn
London

CK Jeanswear
Calvin Klein Inc
Bluewater

CK Jeanswear
Calvin Klein Inc
Hamburg

CK Jeanswear
Calvin Klein Inc
Dubai

Calvin Klein Store
Calvin Klein Inc
Fukuoka

Calvin Klein Men's
Collection
Calvin Klein Inc
Dubai

2000
Calvin Klein Store
Calvin Klein Inc
Taipei

Stewart House
Martha Stewart
Long Island
(in progress)

Harvey Apartment
James Harvey
London
(in progress)

Walsh House
Catherine Walsh
Telluride
(in progress)

Blakstad House
Lucy Blakstad and Adrian
Caddy
London
(in progress)

Wilheim House
John Wilheim
Los Angeles
(in progress)

Ostyn House
Bea and Geert Ostyn
Belgium
(in progress)

250 Brompton Road
Chelsfield Plc
London
(in progress)

Bulthaup Showroom
The Kitchen People
London
(in progress)

Bathroom System
Obumex
Belgium
(in progress)

Cookware Collection
Demeyere
Belgium
(in progress)

Ironmongery Collection
Valli & Valli
Milan
(in progress)

CK Color Cosmetics
Calvin Klein Inc
(in progress)

2001
Maack House
Kamilla and Tim Maack
Germany
(in progress)

Batavia Building
Sodium
Amsterdam
(in progress)

Wardour Castle Apartment
Nigel Tuersley
Wiltshire
(in progress)

2002
Cistercian Monastery
Abbaye Notre-Dame de
Sept Fons
Czech Republic
(in progress)

The Young Vic Theatre
Young Vic Theatre
London
(in progress)

Landsdowne Lodge
Apartments
Grainger Trust
London
(in progress)

Driade Furniture Collection
Driade
Italy
(in progress)

index

Photography:
Aerographics Corp 142;
John Andrews 28; Jonnie
Bell 151; Adam Bartos 144;
Prudence Cummings 19,
22; Richard Davies 128,
188, 189, 208, 210; Ian
Dobbie 10, 13, 14, 25, 33;
Todd Eberle 16, 58, 60, 138,
152, 159, 214, 218, 220,
222, 226, 230; Dennis
Gilbert 97, 108, 110;
Richard Glover 24, 27, 35,
36, 40, 42, 44, 46, 74, 76,
81, 83, 84, 85, 87, 89, 90,
115, 118, 126, 190, 191,
193, 194, 196, 198, 200,
204, 207, 228; Christoph
Kicherer 9, 52, 62, 64, 66,
92, 103;

Enzo Stefano Manola 56;
Fi McGhee 166, 169, 170,
173, 174, 176, 178, 181,
182; Michael Mundy 23
Stéphane Orsolini 38
Nacasa and Partners 48,
67, 68, 71, 72, 100, 104,
106, 116, 184; Cindy
Palmano 202, 238; John
Pawson 26; Charlotte
Williams 209

Digital Images:
Anthony Thistleton 122,
132, 136,154, 160,163

acknowledgements

John Pawson wishes to thank the author Deyan Sudjic and from the architect's office: Simon Dance, Alejandro Fernandez, Andre Fu, Nicole Germann, William Hall, Vishwa Kaushal, Enzostefano Manola, Chris Masson, Virginia McLeod, Alison Morris, Stéphane Orsolini, Pierre Saalburg, Charlotte Williams.

Thanks also to the commissioning editor Anita Moryadas and editor Hannah Barnes-Murphy, Frances Johnson and Paul Hammond at Phaidon Press.

Collaborators include: John Andrews, Richard Baldwin, Jonnie Bell, Arnold Chan, Tom Croft, Jim Hardwick, Richard Hopper, Ian Howe, Clyde Malby, Ian McKay, Crispin Osborne, Sean Perkins, David Rosen, Hester van Royen, Anthony Thistleton, Stephen Quinlan and Denton Corker Marshall.

John Pawson was in partnership with Claudio Silvestrin from 1987 to 1989.

To Catherine, Caius and Benedict Pawson.

Phaidon Press Limited
Regent's Wharf
All Saints Street
London N1 9PA

Phaidon Press Inc.
180 Varick Street
New York, NY 10014

www.phaidon.com

First published 2000
Reprinted 2001
© 2000 Phaidon Press Limited

ISBN 0 7148 3909 4

A CIP catalogue for this book
is available from the British
Library

Designed by
Stephen Wolstenholme
Printed in China